How to Help Children Learn Music

The Singing Staff

How to Help Children Learn Music

by

MADELEINE CARABO-CONE

and

BEATRICE ROYT

PHOTOGRAPHS BY ANN MEUER

With a Section on Fingerboard Ear-Training
by Madeleine Carabo-Cone

HARPER & BROTHERS, NEW YORK

Mt
I
C2.7

CONTENTS

PREFACE

A FEW years ago a young mother and professional musician who had begun her musical training at a tender age, wanted her five-year-old daughter to start piano lessons. So she asked a friend with a background of concert and teaching experience to come to the country and teach her child. But she had not reckoned with the self-propelling forces of modern education. Throughout the lesson, the little darling could be heard complaining, "There's Sally outside. Why do I have to stay in here and take this horrible lesson? I want to play with my friends."

It was soon apparent that the only solution was to bring the friends into the lessons. And so the children's music classes started downstairs in the playroom. Soon the walls and floors were covered with musical drawings and cutouts. The familiar children's games were being translated into musical terms, and new games were developing as musical needs presented themselves. For the youngsters the emphasis was on play, but gradually, and without their realizing it, they were learning basic musical concepts and instrumental techniques.

Here was the pleasure principle at work. Not only were the children having a wonderful time, but they were learning at a faster pace than they could at that age in private lessons. Their learning span of attention had been lengthened by the variety of games; and in a single group hour the teacher was covering many more aspects of music study than the private teacher could cover in a half-hour lesson, with too little time on the teacher's part and too little attention and energy on the pupil's part.

Soon classes for older children were added; new games and new teaching devices were developed. Earlier experience in teaching a variety of children provided additional techniques and materials. The teacher's and the mother's combined academic musical backgrounds and their experiences as performers provided a realistic estimate of the kind of musical equipment necessary for instrumental playing: the ability to read music, the kinesthetic sense of the instrument, the rhythmic sense, the quick response, the strengthened fingers, and so forth. And the more they worked in the cellar playroom the more convinced they became that children could be introduced to all of these things through pleasurable modern educational techniques.

Out of this varied background developed the program of music-through-play that is described in this book. The project was so conceived that musical parents and music teachers everywhere might be able to use it as a basis for teaching groups of their own, enabling children to enjoy music lessons and carrying them over the most difficult period of all—the beginning.

For this is just a beginning. Teaching-through-play is no substitute for the patient, rigorous individual training that must go on if a child is to become a competent instrumentalist. But the beginning is important. So many learning processes and so many delicate and complex coordinations are involved in even the first piano or violin lessons that it is little wonder that children soon become discouraged. If, however, the child's first musical experiences are joyful, if in his musical play his rhythmic, aural, and muscular responses are quickened, the child, fortified with these fundamentals, can go wherever his musical instincts lead him, with the security of a firm foundation.

Although the terms here employed have been kept as simple as possible, they are necessarily based on a certain knowledge of the fundaments of music. For a parent or teacher who wants to introduce children to more than the sound and feeling of music, familiarity with such ideas as clefs, staves, scales, time values, keys, tempo markings, and so forth, is essential. An ability to read simple music and to play scales, chords, and modest pieces on the piano is also necessary, unless the teacher is fortunate enough to have a pianist always at hand. This is not to suggest that the pleasure of music is the exclusive province of the tutored; or that the only way to teach music is through the method described in this book. *How to Help Children Learn Music* is not intended to supplant but rather to supplement materials already in the field—rhythm band work, eurhythmics, group singing, and existing piano methods.

Thus, if there is more about string techniques in this book than is generally found in beginning manuals, it is because there is less material for young children in this field than in any other. The current dearth of string students in advanced music schools and, therefore, of a reservoir of violin, cello, and viola performers for future symphony orchestras is in part a reflection of this fact. The fingerboard materials at the end of this book are an effort to bridge the gap.

Most of the musical games here described require only the simplest improvised materials, which can be devised from the descriptions included in the text. Additional materials—such as the Scale Charts, the Cone-Royt Singing Staff and Practice Keyboard, and certain music especially composed for this method— will soon be available, and information concerning them can be obtained by writing Cone-Royt, c/o Harper & Brothers. In some cases the teacher will want to develop games of her own as variations on those in the text. In this process, if she has done her job well, she will find her pupils willing collaborators, for their music will be their pleasure, and children have always been ingenious inventors of pleasure.

The authors wish to express their appreciation to Dr. Ordway Tead for his independent recognition and strong support of this project; to Mrs. Robert Popper for her generous interest and invaluable editorial assistance; to Mr. Harold S. Cone and Dr. and Mrs. Otto Krash for the performance of those onerous chores that befall members of one's family; to Miss Sharada Pai of New Delhi, India, for bolstering their Clap-touch system with corroborative detail; to the neighbors, friends, and parents of pupils who lent a helpful hand with typewriter, equipment, and paintbrush; and always—to those whose devotion through the years kept a warm glow through the Glacial Period of their early studies and career pursuits.

MADELEINE CARABO-CONE AND BEATRICE ROYT

INTRODUCTION

THE active enjoyment of music derived from personal participation is bound to be a more vital experience than the passive pleasure of uninformed listening. Yet each year thousands of children are denied their natural musical fulfillment by the discouragement of their early studies. So many intricate coordinations are required of them at even their first lessons, so few satisfactions are recognizable, that the strain soon reaches a breaking point and the undertaking is abandoned, often after years of costly lessons under trained musicians and teachers.

Our aim is to relieve all strain, indeed to prevent its appearance, by introducing children to music in an atmosphere of fun and familiarity and participation with friends. Everywhere in the child's daily life he is surrounded by words—words on signs, words on billboards, words on bottles, boxes, and barrels. Words are his natural environment; in all probability, he would sooner or later begin to read them in self-defense. But the symbols of musical language are hieroglyphics to him unless they are first explained with help. In the musical playshop the hieroglyphics of music become as much a part of the child's environment as the hieroglyphics of language are a part of his everyday world. Here, too, games are helpful, for playing with musical symbols soon dispels their strangeness. In a short time the child can recognize the staff, the notes, the clefs, the rests, the signatures. On closer acquaintance, the formal accoutrements of music become as familiar to him as his own coat or hat. His orientation has begun. His head is turned toward the door marked "Music Reading Readiness."

Learning begins for the children of nursery school age when they enter the music "playshop," and see large black paper cutouts of notes and musical symbols that have been thumbtacked or taped to the walls. On their first visit, they engage in

1

a Treasure Hunt, looking for similar cutouts hidden about the room. In elation at each discovery, they match their prizes to the wall decorations. The very search, the physical handling and feeling of the shapes of these symbols is accomplished with glee, the first condition for easy learning. On further visits, the children themselves draw and cut more notes and symbols out of black paper, which in turn can be used in additional games or hidden for more Treasure Hunts.

The party gets into full swing with active games, each game concealing a specific learning process. Interspersed with the physically active games are more quiet, but absorbing, pursuits. Active games follow with a few minutes out for light refreshment. The children come back to the games with renewed energy and, even better, renewed concentration. Time flies, the party is over too soon, and the children reluctantly leave.

During all these free action games, the children sing and listen to pertinent musical sounds that are an integral part of each activity. In this way, the sense of hearing is brought into play.

To bring the child closer and closer to intricate coordinations, we must start through the large muscles. The child needs wide areas for free movement, just as he needs large symbols to handle. And just as we have sent him scurrying about the room looking for the symbols that he can grasp and feel, so we put an immense musical staff on the floor for walking, running, jumping, stepping, beanbag throwing, and other games. We also relate the lines on the staff to the child's own body; the bottom line to his feet, the second to his knees, the third to his waist, the fourth to his shoulders, and the top to his head. The two staffs, the Floor Staff and the Body Staff, are integrated in several games. The same approach of large-muscle free movement and identification of the musical concept with the child's own self is apparent in other devices.

We transmit rhythmic concepts through the same large muscles. A square wooden frame and an equilateral triangle frame are used for the introductory conducting games. The child, with a big, easy-swinging motion of the arm, follows the contour of

2

a square for 4/4 time and the contour of the triangle for 3/4 time. The arm movement is full of freedom but it also contains the element of evenness. Furthermore each completed square or triangle movement is a demonstration of a completed measure expressed in time and in space.

In another game, the arm imitates the oscillation of the pendulum, again using large, relaxed, easy-swinging movements to music, emphasizing the pendulum concept of rhythm. We teach rhythm as a living pulsation, not as a rigid and often not-too-regular counting.

The pulsation concept of rhythm is a universal law that governs nature and art. The expansion and contraction of the heart, the undulation of the waves, the ebb and flow of the tide, the strong and weak beats of poetry, the succession of solids and voids in architecture—all bear witness to the underlying principle of rhythm as a pulsation. Children are fascinated by these phenomena; the teacher points them out constantly and tries whenever possible to parallel them with musically descriptive examples. The children imitate the rhythmic movement in their daily surroundings—the see-saw, the swing, wagging puppytails, the horse's trot; they feel their pulses, mark the strong and weak beats of poetry, and compose strongly accented jingles of their own.

From the free-swinging games, the child proceeds to a graphic measurement of note values and the construction of rhythmic patterns of notes, again measuring the patterns in space as well as in time. Then, carrying out the cardinal principle of total motor involvement, we help him interpret note values in singing, singing while walking, running, skipping, and stepping, clapping devices, and combinations of all of these, interspersed with a direct instrumental application.

At this point we introduce small violins and cellos. With some assistance at first in holding the bow, the child can readily translate his measured steps, his singing and clapping, into the same rhythmically measured bowings on one open string. He begins with one measure, which is soon extended to the most common musical unit, the four-measure phrase. When each member of the group is given a turn with the string instruments, it is not unlikely that a few conversions to the string section will have begun. Even for those with a steadfast preference for the keyboard this is not waste motion. (A renowned artist used to say that every pianist should begin with some lessons on the violin in order to learn the meaning of a sustained tone.) The fact that pianists and string players number their fingers differently causes no confusion on the open string, where fingering is not involved.

Through the visual-aural-muscular coordinations; through the strengthening finger games; the early introduction of scales in all tonalities to prevent the formation of mental blocks about "difficult keys"; and, above all, through the emphasis on a kinesthetic, "touch-system" sense of the instrument, we slowly, but inevitably, lay the groundwork for an efficient instrumental technique. With this equipment the child is also prepared to develop a sight-reading efficiency that will provide increasing satisfaction throughout his lifetime.

Children can derive great pleasure from playing by rote, but alas, this pleasure is short-lived and often leads to frustration when the child discovers that he cannot cope with the multitudinous coordinations required when he comes to reading music. One child who had had several years of piano study, carried on mainly by imitation of the teacher, gave up her lessons when she was confronted with printed music. Although she could read books with speed and understanding, she was exasperated by music reading that required not only the visual sense but a coordinated kinesthetic sense of the instrument—a transference from the printed page to the fingers, ears, rhythmic sense, and other physical and mental involvements.

Comparison between primer reading books and primer music books reveals a shocking difference. In a reading primer, there may be one word repeated several times on a single page— "look . . . look . . . look," or "oh . . . oh . . . oh"—but "oh, look" at a typical music primer!—five or ten lines, bass clef, treble clef, quarter notes, half notes, time signatures (not to mention paragraphs of instruction for the teacher), all strange

4

symbols to the child, none of them possessing the personal meaning of even a familiar word.

From the beginning, we endeavor to make these symbols a part of the child's environment. We take advantage of the fact that nothing is more familiar to the child than his own self. From allowing the child to identify himself with both the staff and the keyboard in games involving the large muscles, we progress gradually to activities that begin to use the smaller muscles —copying music, for example, on large staves with checkers for notes. At all times, there is a constant stress on patterns—patterns to see, patterns to hear, and patterns to demonstrate in games and at the instrument. The first connection between the played notes and the visual score is thus secured.

Then through the quiet concentration of a scroll-reading device, the child's vision is directed into a small area and suspense is created by the slow and rhythmic unfurling of the scroll which, in itself, is a demonstration of rhythm in both time and space. The whole image of bass and treble staff together, though vertical in itself, approximates a single word in a horizontal left-to-right reading. The focus is intensified and the reading simplified because all the distractions of the surrounding measures are removed. Moreover, the child's attention is so riveted to the scroll and he is so eager for the next revelation that he cannot remove his eyes for a moment to look down at the keyboard, but plays what he sees with almost hypnotic ease. Involuntarily he is achieving complete concentration and therefore complete coordination.

"Practice makes perfect" and "Repetition is the best instructor" are maxims that are emblazoned on the music racks of every professional musician. But the child reared in the permissive and developmental ways of today will not learn a word merely by writing it a hundred times on the blackboard; on the contrary, he will store up an unforgettable rage against it. If, however, the child is brought into personal contact with a word that has been made meaningful and useful, the impression will be lasting.

Even in play, the necessary musical tasks and primary materials must be gone over dozens of times; the child must make direct

5

use of the material over and over again. But we must take care that he is not bored by the repetition. The teacher must be on the alert for novel ways of presenting the same material in such a fresh way that the sameness is indiscernible. Through the various motor involvements of the child, we must introduce him to the materials of music in so many different guises that the teacher can safely expect at least one approach to enter through at least one channel.

The games and activities described in the following chapters begin with the simplest and progress steadily toward the more complex. Many of the projects are suitable for children up to twelve years old. In each game the focus is on the isolation of one new learning process; and for each learning process, several related variations are presented. At each class it is possible to use only a selected few of these games. Sample lesson plans (see Appendix C) are derived from one teacher's experience, but these are intended only as suggestions. Sessions should never be fixed into a rigid routine, but combined in a constantly varying and lively program.

Furthermore, in devising and presenting the games to the children, it is essential that all of the trappings be relevant; they must also be unobtrusive; the fantasy must be an interpretation of the actual learning problem. Play is the method, but it should never be forgotten by the teacher that music is the point.

Nor should it be forgotten that the musical experience is more than the bits and pieces that make it up. Even as we try to develop concentration and coordination, and continue to familiarize the child with the fundaments of music, we cannot neglect to cast a constant glimmer on form, structure, poise, and pulse—the eternal verities of all art. The child will never feel that he is in the dark if he can cling to these supports. He needs their security if only to compensate for his technical inadequacy in the early years of study.

Given these basic tenets of a musical faith, he will gain comfort and patience to sustain him as he works his way through the obstacles that may beset him in the years ahead. He need not turn back, for he will possess the strength and security to seek out for himself the great musical adventure.

GAMES AND ACTIVITIES

Fig. 1. Treasure Hunt

INTRODUCTORY GAMES

Treasure Hunt

MATERIALS: Large treble clefs, bass clefs, whole notes, half notes, and quarter notes cut out of black paper or wood; a basket to hold an assortment of these cutouts; shelf paper marked with treble and bass staves, with notes drawn in with heavy black crayon or felt nib pen.

AS EACH child enters the room he picks a musical cutout from the basket. When he looks about, he sees many similar symbols tacked or taped to the walls. Holding his own paper cutout, he runs to the walls and tries to find its match. Then he engages in a hunt around the room for additional hidden cutouts. At each discovery, the child matches his findings to the symbols on the wall (Fig. 1).

In his wanderings he sees some of the shelf-paper staves mounted on the walls around the room. Without being told in so many words, he has already begun to see the transition from the cutout paper symbol to the written symbol on a sheet of music.

Clef Bracelets

MATERIALS: Pipe cleaners; rubber bands.

The youngest group like to make bass and treble clefs out of pipe cleaners (Fig. 2). They can manage the bass by themselves because they see it as a curling worm. The treble clef, however, must be made with some assistance from the teacher.

When the clefs are finished, each child deposits his bass clef at the lower end of the keyboard, striking a few bass notes with his left hand as he leaves his handiwork. Then each brings his treble clef to the upper part of the keyboard, this time hitting a few high notes with his right hand.

9

Fig. 2. Clef Bracelets

The next week, after the children bend the clefs into shape, we help each one attach the bass clef to his left wrist and the treble clef to his right wrist with brightly colored rubber bands. Again the children go to the piano and play a few bass notes with their left hands, a few treble notes with their right hands. In this way they are introduced to the connection between the treble clef and high notes, played with the right hand, and between the bass clef and low notes, played with the left hand.

A girl of six developed a variation of this game by herself. She laid ten pipe cleaners down horizontally for two staves, placed her treble clef on the top five lines and her bass clef on the bottom, curled one end of a pipe cleaner for a half note, and began to move it from line to space. Spurred on by her contribution, we helped her develop her game: by tightly curling one end of a long pipe cleaner in spiral fashion, we approximated the solid effect of a quarter note; by leaving off the stem of the half note, a whole note was easily fashioned.

10

Notebook Coloring and Drawing

MATERIALS: 12″ x 18″ sketching tablets; colored crayons.

Each child is given a tablet and crayons in which he draws and colors for a short while at each of the first "musical parties."

At the first session, the child folds a page of the sketching tablet in half horizontally. The teacher helps the child trace the outline of his left hand on the bottom half of the sheet and of his right hand on the top half. She then draws a bass staff over the left hand and a treble staff over the right. Tracing their hands is an old stunt which always delights children. Used in this way, however, it has special musical applications: first, by correlating the left hand with the bass staff and the right hand with the treble; second, by suggesting, in the fold of the paper, the invisible leger line of middle C.

At another session, the teacher draws a large musical symbol— a note or a clef, or perhaps a sharp or a flat—on the sketchbook page in yellow crayon. The child is given a box of crayons and draws over the symbol several times, each time using a different colored crayon. Each color produces a new effect, and the completed symbol looks as if it had been embroidered in multicolored thread, making the entire notebook a possession which the child will treasure.

At other times, the child draws hills and then draws little figures going up and down. Again, the musical application follows rapidly when, with the teacher's help, the figures become notes, and staff lines are added to mark their progress.

Numerous variations on the musical coloring game can be added as the children's knowledge increases.

Fig. 3. Garden Seed Game

Garden Seed Game

The children pretend they are seeds in the ground that grow toward the sun and then return to the ground. Each winter they shift in the ground and come up a few inches away the next spring (Fig. 3).

The teacher plays the first five notes of the C-major scale on the piano, ascending and then descending, each time holding the fifth note for four beats. The children kneel curled up on the floor. To the notes of the ascending scale they rise and lift their arms upward; on the descending scale, they return to the floor. At the same time they sing:

Rise up to the sun Drop down one by one

All the children shift a few inches to the right, as the key shifts to D-flat major, and the song is repeated. The game continues, the music a half-step higher each time, the children a few inches to the right.

This game is a dramatization of changing keys and of ascending and descending scale motifs. At the same time it is an exercise in ear-training in which the whole body participates. After a few sessions, the concept of loud and soft can be introduced, with the children singing louder as the scale ascends, softer as it—and they—descend. The dynamics can also be varied from time to time, with the singing all loud, or all soft, or moving from loud to soft and back to loud.

Fig. 4. Conducting Frames

RHYTHM AND PULSATION

Conducting

MATERIALS: 18″ square and equilateral triangle frames, made of wood or cardboard, or of wire hangers bent into shape.

Each child is given a square frame, which he holds in his left hand, top center (or by the hook, if wire hangers are used). While music is played in 4/4 time, the child, starting in the upper left-hand corner, follows the interior outline of the square with his hand or pencil, down, across, up, and back, touching each successive corner sharply, one to a beat (Fig. 4, top). Each completed movement around the square gives the child the concept of the total measure. The arm movement is free and relaxed, but it is also even, like the musical beat.

For 2/4 time he slides his pencil down one side and up again for a measure. For 3/4 time an equilateral triangle is used (Fig. 4, bottom); and 6/8 time calls for two triangular motions for each measure.

Grandfather Clock Game

MATERIALS: *Tape measures that unwind and spring back into small round metal containers.*

Pendulums can be made of the tapes by extending them to a given distance and swinging them from the tape end, with the container as the weight. By lengthening or shortening the tape, differences in tempo can be demonstrated—faster with a shorter tape, slower with a longer one (Fig. 5, top).

Children find it difficult to distinguish between tempo, which relates to the over-all speed of a piece, and meter, which relates to the time values and accent patterns of notes within a measure, at any given tempo. Often a child will say, for example, "An eighth note is a fast note, isn't it?" It is easy to demonstrate with the improvised pendulum that quarter notes sung to a quick swing, or tempo, may be faster than eighth notes sung to a slow tempo.

Once the principle of the pendulum is understood, the children are ready for the Grandfather Clock Game. Whispering "tick-tock, tick-tock," each child swings his right arm like a pendulum to the accompaniment of victrola records or rhythmic piano music (Fig. 5, bottom). Once the even swing is established, the pianist can begin to slow up or rush. The children will laugh as their pendulums go out of order and they become aware, through their arms, of the faulty rhythm.

The pendulum concept is useful, first because the rhythmic swing is accomplished through the large muscles which are the easiest for the child to control, and second because it inculcates in the beginner the idea of pulsation—of rhythmic ebb and flow—rather than beat. Just like the human pulse, music is a continuous alternation of strong and weak accents, rather than a mechanical progression from stress to stress, as the emphasis on beat implies. Children are never too young to be introduced to the principle of pulsation.

It is a common fault of beginning instrumentalists—children and adults alike—to halt at each measure line, and to rush the

Fig. 5. Grandfather Clock Game

easy passage and slow down for the difficult one. Yet even a child, when he begins to learn a new piece, should be able to find a tempo that will enable him to perform the most difficult passage without slowing down. (As great a musician as Toscanini told his friend Adolfo Betti that he found his touchstone for tempo settings in the most florid or complex passage of the composition.) Once established, the tempo will be maintained if the performer has been thoroughly imbued with a feeling for rhythmic pulsation.

The Grandfather Clock Game should be played with varying rhythms and musical accompaniments each time the group meets. In the early stages 2/4 and 4/4 time is all that should be attempted; as the children become more advanced they can manage the coordination necessary to swing their pendulums to 3/4, 6/8, and more elaborate time schemes.

Rocking-chair Game

MATERIALS: A small rocking chair and a Cone-Royt Singing Staff. The Singing Staff is a stringed instrument made to look like a musical staff, in which the lines—or strings—are tuned to the notes they represent on the staff: GBDFA in the bass clef, EGBDF in the treble. (See Frontispiece and detailed instructions for making the Singing Staff on page 105.)

The children take turns rocking in the chair, while they sing to a tune of quarter notes—G-e G-e—repeated for four measures. They begin the game singing:

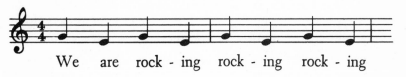

We   are   rock - ing   rock - ing   rock - ing

Soon they are encouraged to invent words of their own. Even nonsense syllables will do, so long as the strong and weak syllables alternate as they do in the motion of rocking and in the word itself. The Rocking-chair Game is another demonstration of musical pulsation, which the smallest child can understand and enjoy.

If a Singing Staff is available, the teacher can accompany the game by plucking the second and first (G and E) lines of the treble staff in time to the song. When the game is repeated another day, a different combination of notes is used, until all the lines of both staves have been played. In this way the children are gradually introduced to the sounds that correspond to each of the lines on the printed staff.

The "Metro-gnome"

MATERIALS: A metronome.

The Grandfather Clock and Rocking Chair games are excellent preparations for the use of the metronome, itself a valuable tool in advanced study for technical and rhythmic discipline. Many accomplished artists use it to develop speed and accuracy in their practicing, but if it is wrongly used, the player finds its insistent beat frustrating and soon abandons it. For this reason, few students ever learn how to use it successfully.

The secret of using a metronome lies in listening to it in silence until its mechanical beat has become one with the player's inner sense of rhythmic pulsation. Two-measures-for-nothing before one begins to play to the metronome are essential for establishing the rhythmic poise—the indispensable sense of rhythmic equilibrium—that permits the proper musical flow.

When the children are old hands at the earlier games, the teacher sets the metronome on the table. The children swing their arms, "following the leader," as they imitate the swing of the metronome to musical accompaniment. The teacher moves the weight on the instrument up and down and the children swing to its different tempi. Each time, before they begin to swing with the metronome, they listen for two measures, until the metronome beat seems one with their own. In this way they soon learn to make the metronome their servant instead of their master, and guarantee that any future use of that instrument will be easy and helpful, rather than irritating and profitless.

Bell Game

MATERIALS: *A metronome with a bell which can be set to indicate the beginning of each measure in any given tempo; a desk bell, such as a teacher uses, which can be rung by hitting the clapper with the palm of the hand; conducting frames.*

The children sit in a circle around a table. In the center the teacher places a metronome with a bell set to ring after every four beats. "How many ticks do you hear after the bell rings?" she asks. From time to time she adjusts the bell to ring after two, three, four or six beats, each time asking the children to count the number of beats.

This is just a warm-up. Now the desk bell is brought to the table. Each child in turn is given a chance to imitate the metronome by tapping the beats on the table in time to the instrument and accompanying music, striking the bell at the first beat of each measure. They begin with a series of two-beat measures, then three-beat, then four-beat, and so forth. The other children sway in their seats in time to the music, or conduct in the frames they have already used for the Conducting Game.

PRINTING-SET STAFF

MATERIALS: Sheets of paper or, preferably, cardboard, 18" x 24"; a toy printing set; ink pads.

Children enjoy playing with a printing set, and used in the following way, this agreeable occupation has a musical application as well.

The teacher begins by pencilling in lightly—or showing the child how to do so—two staves as large as the drawing surface will permit. With crayon, a bass and a treble clef are drawn into place. Beginning with the bottom line, the child stamps the corresponding letter repeatedly from one end to the other on each of the pencilled staff lines (Fig. 6). With a little practice, he can place the letters in any single line so close together that from a distance they appear to flow into one solid line.

A large Printing-set Staff can be used for many of the staves described on the following pages, for example, the Floor Staff, the Staff Puzzle, and the backdrop for the game of Pin the Note on the Staff. It can also be set up as a helper beside the Floor Staff (see, for example, Figs. 9 and 10). Below is a more elaborate version.

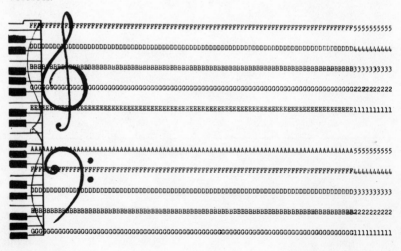

Fig. 6. Printing-set Staff

FLOOR STAFF GAMES

MATERIALS: An old 9' x 12' linoleum rug; white deck paint and black enamel paint; shellac.

The Floor Staff provides the background for many of the musical games which follow, beginning with those contained in this section for the youngest group, and progressing to more difficult ones for older or more advanced students. The Floor Staff should, if possible, be permanently installed in the music playroom. To make it, the linoleum is covered with two coats of white deck paint. Then black enamel lines are painted horizontally across the surface to make the two five-line staves which, bracketed together, form the Grand Staff. A light pencil line is drawn through the center of the space between the two staves to indicate the invisible leger line of middle C. The bass and treble clefs are painted into place at the extreme left, and the whole is covered with several coats of clear shellac. (See, for example, Figs. 7 through 10.) All the Floor Staff games are performed to appropriate musical accompaniment, either on the Singing Staff or on the piano. Thus gradually the children begin to associate each space and each line of the staff with its sound.

Fig. 7. Tightrope Walk

Tightrope Walk

The children imitate circus performers on the Floor Staff, with each line in succession representing the rope (Fig. 7). Lining up to the left of the bottom (G) line of the bass staff, they follow the leader across it, one foot in front of the other, their arms outstretched for balance. While they walk, they hum the sound of the line (an octave above, if necessary) to the teacher's piano accompaniment. When they come off the Floor Staff at the end of the line, they walk around the outside of the staff counterclockwise, and begin the next line (B), again from the left. They proceed this way through the ten lines of the staff, and the invisible C-line. As they walk the tightrope, ear-training is going on unobtrusively, along with staff learning.

A similar game of Trudging through the Snow can be played in the spaces.

Black Lines and White Squares

MATERIALS: *Black and white paper cutouts to correspond to the lines and spaces of the Floor Staff. The white paper cutouts should be squares the size of the distance between two lines on the Floor Staff. The black paper strips should be the same length as the squares but only as wide as the painted lines on the Floor Staff.*

The nursery group enjoys matching the black strips of paper to the black lines of the Floor Staff, the white squares of paper to the spaces. This simple puzzle is one more way of familiarizing them with the staff, and introduces the notion that the spaces between the lines will be as important as the lines themselves. If there is a staircase handy the cutouts can be laid out alternately on the stairs. Then the children walk up and down the stairs to ascending and descending music.

Bug Game

MATERIALS: *Black paper and scissors; safety pins.*

The nursery group cuts out large black paper ovals. Then each child has one pinned to his back as he pretends to be a bug, crawling up the Floor Staff, to music as always (Fig. 8). Then the group is divided into line bugs and space bugs. The line bugs must always be on a line when the music stops, the space bugs on a space. In a variation of this game, line bugs begin at the left and traverse the entire length of a line, beginning again on the next line, as in the Tightrope Walk. At the same time, space bugs traverse each space in succession.

Fig. 8. Bug Game

Trucks on Highways

MATERIALS: *Toy trucks.*

The children push toy trucks to music, along the lines of the Floor Staff, which are now highways. They observe the rules for one-way traffic, beginning each line at the left, coming off the staff at the right, and circling it counterclockwise to begin the next line. With a large number of children, where the circling might cause confusion, each child can be assigned a particular "highway"—or line. Then as the first child comes off the bottom line, the second will begin across the next, and so on up the staff, with the music following them all the way.

Boats on Rivers

MATERIALS: *Toy boats.*

The spaces in the Floor Staff are rivers. The children push their toy boats along the rivers in the same manner as in the truck game.

Shuffleboard

MATERIALS: *Yardsticks, black paper cutouts of notes.*

With a yardstick, each child pushes a black paper note across the Floor Staff. A child plays the "caller," and if the caller yells "line," the pusher must land his note onto a line; if the caller yells "space," the note must land on a space.

As the children progress to learning the names of the notes, the caller can yell a specific note—such as G—and the pusher is "safe" so long as he puts his note on any G on the staff.

Beanbag Game

MATERIALS: *Oval beanbags made of textured black cloth, or of white cloth edged with an oval strip of black cloth to resemble a whole note.*

The young child throws the beanbag at the staff, calling "line" if it lands on a line, or "space" if it lands on a space (Fig. 9). If he can call his throw correctly and, above all, instantaneously, he gets a second throw. This is an early approach to the reflex-action response that will be of utmost importance for instrumental technique and sight-reading efficiency.

With older children who are beginning to learn the names of the lines and spaces, the teacher places a Printing-set Staff upright near the Floor Staff where everyone can see it. The child then wins another chance to throw if he calls the name of the line or space on which his beanbag has landed. The standing staff is more than a crutch, for it serves to remind the children that although the Floor Staff is horizontal, the musical staff it represents is vertical on the printed page. As the children gain experience this lettered staff can be removed. Again, reflex-action speed in calling the names of the notes should be the aim.

Fig. 9. Beanbag Game

BODY OR LIVE STAFF GAMES

MATERIALS: Paper cutouts of notes; crude brown-paper cutouts of a gingerbread boy and girl, each made to fit five lines of the Floor Staff; Singing Staff.

In order to make the staff as familiar to the child as possible, the teacher relates it to the parts of the child's own body. His feet represent the bottom line, his knees the second line, his waist the middle line, his shoulders the fourth line, and the top of his head the fifth line (Fig. 10). This is his Body or Live Staff, and it corresponds to the GBDFA lines of the bass or the EGBDF lines of the treble. In the early stages, it is enough if the children can get the feeling of moving up and down the Body Staff by appropriate stages as the music moves up and down the staves. The spaces are not stressed until later, since it

Fig. 10. Body Staff

is the lines that serve as anchor points for the eyes and can be most speedily recognized.

Each child hides a note behind his back. The teacher or one of the pupils calls "bottom line," and points to the G-line in the bass clef of the Floor Staff. Quick as a flash, each child whisks out his note and holds it to his feet. In this way the game progresses through each note of both staves, the children holding their paper notes to the corresponding parts of their bodies each time. As the notes are called the teacher plucks the appropriate string on the Singing Staff.

To make the game more vivid, the gingerbread cutouts are superimposed on the staff, the girl on the treble, the boy on the bass. At holiday time, the gingerbread children can be replaced with different motifs: skeletons for Halloween, Santa Claus for Christmas, and so forth. In each case, the arms, knees, waist, shoulders, and head of the cutout rest on the appropriate lines. These serve as reminders of the Body Staff and as attention-getting devices, but it should always be clear that they are temporary and serve no musical function.

In dealing with the staff, it is important that the G-line and not the A-line of the bass staff always be considered the "first" line. Numbering the lines and spaces of every musical staff from the bottom up merely follows their rising alphabetical order. (Those who refer to the top (A) line of the bass staff as the first do so, however, with good intentions since it is the first line encountered downward from middle C, and middle C is presented as a first note in many piano primers.)

Moreover, the base of the musical chord is fundamental. The overtones developed from sounding the bass form all of the chords and the entire harmonic fabric of our music. It was a common practice for seventeenth- and eighteenth-century composers to indicate chords in their compositions instead of writing them out. They did this by writing the bottom note of the chord with an identifying figure above or below it (the figured bass). Any musician could fill out the composer's intentions by reading the instructions in the numbers of the figured bass, and that meant reading up from the bottom. Hence the additional importance of thinking of the bottom G of the bass staff as its first line.

Pin the Note on the Staff

MATERIALS: A large white sheet, marked with a Printing-set Staff, on which a gingerbread child has been lightly drawn into the position of the Body Staff on each clef; cutout notes; safety pins.

That surefire success of any children's party—Pin the Tail on the Donkey—is given a musical twist in Pin the Note on the Staff. Each child is given a note with a safety pin attached. Blindfolded, he tries to pin the note on one of the lines or spaces (Fig. 11). For each round, the line or space is picked in advance by the children.

Fig. 11. Pin the Note on the Staff

COMBINATIONS OF FLOOR STAFF
AND BODY STAFF

Parade of the Acrobats

The children line up parallel to the bottom line of the Floor Staff, and walk up the staff. Starting at the bottom line G, they step into space A, then line B, and so on all the way to the top. When the children come to the pencilled line on the Floor Staff which indicates middle C, they step into the space below this almost invisible line, onto the line, and then above it to get to the first line (E) of the treble. They are accompanied by scale-like music, and gradually they begin to sing the letter names as they go. As they walk, they bring the Body Staff into play by placing their hands on their feet at the first line, knees at the second, and so on through all the different positions.

When the children reach the top of the treble staff they walk backward down the staff and down the scale. This is important since for descending scales they must be able to think of the letter names backward.

Statues

"Statues" has always been a childhood favorite. Children love to run and then freeze into positions. The surprise and suspense of the "stop-the-music" element in Musical Chairs is another special delight. The musical version of the Statue Game combines these two features. The children run up the staff lightly to a rapid ascending scale played on the piano. They must step on each line and each space going up, and must do the same as they run backward down the staff. When the music stops abruptly, the children must freeze into the Body Staff position required by the line or space on which they find themselves. The spaces can be indicated on intermediate parts of the body (leg, thigh, chest, and face).

This game is a boon to the teacher if the children are bursting with energy and need release.

33

Gingerbread Staff Children

The combination of Floor Staff and Body Staff can also provide restful games, if the children are tired. For the Gingerbread Staff Game, each child pretends he is a gingerbread boy or girl and lies down on the Floor Staff so that his feet are approximately at the bottom line, knees at the second line, and so forth. It is an anatomical miracle that children from three to six are able to fit their Body Staffs to the Floor Staff in this way without difficulty.

Once on the floor the children let their imaginations carry them right into the staff. For the youngest children it is enough of a "game" if the teacher places a black paper note on the "lines" of their Body Staffs. Or she can play various notes on the piano, while the children wriggle the parts of their bodies that correspond to the musical sound. These are only two of the variety of quiet games that can be played while the children are taking their rest on the Floor Staff.

One-red-line Flash Cards

MATERIALS: *A series of flash cards of the treble and bass staves, with one of the staff lines drawn in red, a different one on each card.*

The teacher flashes a card, and the children quickly run to the same line on the Floor Staff, at the same time touching the appropriate part of their Body Staff. Immediate reaction is important.

FLOWER GARDEN STAFF

MATERIALS: Flowers made of seven different colors of crepe paper with wires for stems; two "scarecrow" markers with some resemblance to clefs, similarly contrived; and a peg-board of perforated soundproofing material, into which the flowers can be set into rows like the musical staves (Petalcraft, which is available in hobby stores, contains the necessary equipment for the Flower Garden Staff. If these or similar materials are not available, the variously colored flowers and the scarecrows can be painted on a piece of cardboard); a small watering can or pitcher.

The staff is set up by the teacher with successive rows of flowers, each one indicating by its initial the letter name of the staff line. Thus the bass staff begins with Geraniums, then Begonias, Daisies, Forget-me-nots, Asters; the treble with Evergreens, Geraniums, Begonias, Daisies, and Forget-me-nots. A row of Carnations is added between the two staves to make middle C. (These should be white to emphasize the special nature of the C-line.) A scarecrow is set in place of each of the usual clefs: next to the Forget-me-not row in the bass, and next to the Geranium row in the treble.

The teacher is the head gardener, the children her helpers. She instructs each one in turn to water five rows of the garden, each time specifying the position of the G-line or the F-line. Thus, at first, she instructs a child to water five rows, being sure that the Forget-me-nots are the fourth row from the bottom; another must be sure that Geraniums are the second row from the bottom. Then gradually they move around the staff, watering five rows each time, with the Geranium line as the first, second, third, fourth, or fifth line from the bottom, the Forget-me-not line as the first, second, third, or fourth.

In this way the children begin to achieve the necessary flexibility to be able to use a part of the staff, but always in the context of the whole. At the same time, they are identifying the bass clef as the F-clef, the treble as the G. An observant child is also likely to notice the repetition of Begonias, Daisies, and For-

35

get-me-nots in both staves, which is an opportunity for the teacher to point out that the similarity extends to their sounds as well.

Later on, the Flower Garden Staff can also serve as an introduction to the C-clefs used by violas and violoncellos. A third marker is placed next to the Carnation line and, in the course of the game, a child is told to water five rows, being sure that Carnations are the third row from the bottom. The worker, watering F, A, middle C, E, and G, is encompassing the lines of the alto staff. Another child watering five rows with Carnations the fourth row from the bottom, is covering the lines of the tenor staff—D, F, A, middle C, and E. With the preparation of the earlier version of the game, this concept of the two C-clefs, which has been a stumbling block for many advanced musicians, will not be difficult for children to understand. When, as advanced students, they come to a study of string instruments, the memory of the Flower Garden Staff will serve as a vivid introduction to the special provinces of the viola and cello.

FINGER GAMES

The early finger games are all done at the table, where one learning process at a time can be isolated and slowly worked into a combination of coordinations. A child can learn to respond to the numbers of his fingers with reflex speed under the stimulation of games, and when, physically and psychologically, he is relaxed because he is enjoying himself. Too many children become tense and self-conscious during piano and violin lessons when the teacher criticizes their hand position while they are so valiantly struggling with innumerable other problems. They tighten up their hands if even so much as a mention of hand position is made. At the table, the child has the relaxed opportunity to concentrate on the strength of the tip of his fingers, the tunnel under his knuckles, and the arch of the hand, without the added complexities of pushing and finding keys. In time the correct hand position becomes second nature.

Many of the Finger Games can also be done on a foam rubber "exercise mat" which is an effective finger strengthener and also a surface that children enjoy. This can be a plain strip of foam rubber or a black-and-white "keyboard." (See description of Cone-Royt Practice Keyboard, page 107, and Fig. 30.)

Pick Up Sticks

MATERIALS: Pencils.

Each child picks up a pencil from a collection in the center of the table (Fig. 12, top). The hand is relaxed; there is just enough control to keep the pencil from falling. The child observes his hand after it has picked up the pencil. He can see that his fingers are curved, his knuckles arched, his whole arm completely relaxed so that he can roll, swing, or slowly shake his wrist and elbow while the pencil remains in his light grasp. This is equally important for the piano hand position and for string instrument bowing.

Fig. 12. Finger Games: top, Pick Up Sticks; bottom, Cotton Picking

Hanging On to the Boat

The children gather around a table pretending that they are in the water. The imaginary inflated rubber boat in which they have been playing has spilled them out; as they move about freely in the water, their fingers hold onto the edge of the table, or "boat." Their arms, wrists, and elbows rotate freely in the choppy waters, while their fingers hang on firmly. The teacher walks around and tries to brush or pull their fingers off the boat; on her second attempt she usually fails. By "hanging on to the boat" the children are learning the combination of firm fingers and flexible arms and wrists which are necessary equipment for the pianist.

Cotton Picking

MATERIALS: Round puffs of cotton, 2" in diameter.

Each child lifts a cotton ball from the table (Fig. 12, bottom). He has an immediate sensation of lightness. His fingers are curved, his knuckles arched, and there is no tightness along his arm or hand. He takes the cotton ball to the piano and observes his hand position on the keys, still keeping the cotton in his palm. In this simple fashion, he has learned the proper hand position which so many small music students learn only with difficulty.

Parade of the Fingers

MATERIALS: Small toy trucks.

    Back at the table, the children prepare for the Parade of the Fingers. As they get their hands into "cotton" position, the teacher runs the toy trucks under their arched knuckles saying, "This is a very tall truck and needs a high tunnel" (Fig. 13). If the children get their wrists too high, she runs the toy truck up their forearms calling for a level highway, the Jersey turnpike, or something of the sort.

Fig. 13. Parade of the Fingers

Now comes the parade itself. The fingers are a troupe of circus performers "warming up." The first and second fingers march as everyone sings, "Marching, marching, see the gay parade." They listen for the sound of "drums" as the "drum" of each finger hits the table. Every now and then the toy truck whizzes under the knuckle tunnels, to keep them in position.

Next the second and third fingers march; then the first three fingers, one-two-three and one-two-three. Then the children learn to skip one finger by marching with the first and third. In the early sessions, the children acquire control of the first three fingers and, at the end of each lesson they can be taught a simple piece involving just these fingers. Most elementary piano books contain such material.

In the following weeks, the weaker fourth and fifth fingers are developed in the same manner. When all the fingers have marched, they are ready for the Dance of the Fingers and the Five-finger Waltz Duets.

Dance of the Fingers

Each finger wants to dance with every other finger. The dance begins with the fifth and fourth fingers. Each finger in turn steps and bows to a half note, two step-bows to a measure. Then they walk, walk, walk, walk, five-four-five-four to quarter notes. Finally, they are running, running, running, running in pairs of eighth notes.

On one day the fifth finger dances with all the other fingers as partners. On another day, the fourth finger dances, four-five, four-three, four-two, four-one. Following lessons give all the other fingers a chance to dance with each other, step-bowing, walking, and running. Even the thumb wants to have every finger as a partner.

Here is a valuable trill exercise in three different rhythms for all types of fingering, presented in a manner that can be understood by a five-year-old.

41

Schumann Says (Simon Says)

The important element in this musical version of Simon Says is the cultivation of the lightning response. The children hold their hands behind their backs (they always enjoy this secretive gesture). The teacher calls, "Simon says, 'First finger, right hand,'"—or "Simon says, 'Second finger, left hand,'" and so forth—and the children hold up the appropriate finger. There must be an instantaneous and correct response. However, the objective is to keep all the children in the game, so no one is ever eliminated for an error.

Since pianists call their thumbs the first finger, while the index finger is the "first" for instrumentalists, this game is only appropriate for children who are studying the same instrument

INTRODUCTION TO THE KEYBOARD

MATERIALS: Upright piano; white paper.

The first thing a father usually does when he takes his child for a ferryboat ride is to show him the engine room. The father knows that the child is unable to understand the mechanics of the engine room, but will be stimulated by the sight of the inner workings. In taking the child for a trip on the Good Ship Keyboard the teacher can also show him the "engine room" by removing the cover of an upright piano. The child will not understand the physics or the engineering, but he will be impressed, and he can acquire in this way certain important musical information.

When the child's curiosity is sufficiently aroused, the teacher can explain and demonstrate that when he presses a key, he moves a hammer which in turn strikes a string. The key is but the handle of the hammer. Each child may have a turn touching the string while its key is struck by the teacher or another child. "Oh, this tickles," he will usually exclaim. "Why does it tickle?" asks the teacher. "It is vibrating," someone may volunteer.

In order to show that the white and black keys are all the same distance (a half step) apart, the teacher covers up the part of the white keys that extends beyond the black notes on the keyboard with a long strip of white paper, leaving only the inner 3¾" visible. As the child strikes each key, he soon realizes that, whether the keys are white or black, the hammers look alike inside.

Keyboard Puzzle

MATERIALS: Sheets of white cardboard, 6½″ long and 5¾″ wide (the distance on the piano from C to B, inclusive) with six 2″ slits along one side to mark the divisions between the white keys; strips of black and white paper to resemble keys, cut from a pattern made by tracing the keyboard, with an extra half inch at the back to fold and clip over the edge of the cardboard; clips.

The teacher hands each child a Keyboard Puzzle, with the five black keys clipped into place like the black notes between C and B on the piano. She asks, "What is this? . . . What colors do you see? . . . Do the black keys stand next to one another?" She points out the groups of two and of three black keys, and reminds the children of the hammers they have just seen inside the piano. Next she explains that the division of the keyboard into black and white keys, and the grouping of black keys into two's and three's, help show the way around the piano.

Now the children sit at a table and are given the Keyboard Puzzle with the black strips removed by the teacher and placed in the center of the table. The teacher shows a sample of the puzzle with the black notes in place and asks the children again to count the number of black keys. When they answer "Five," she tells them to take five black strips and clips. This act impresses upon the children the number of black keys in the octave.

They are now asked to assemble the puzzle by fastening the black strips to their keyboards, folding the creased half inch over the back of the cardboard in order to clip it on securely (Fig. 14, top). "Where to clip them?" All eyes look more sharply as the children make frequent visits to the piano keyboard (Fig. 14, center). They now see that five of the lines that divide the white keys of their puzzle are covered by black keys and they also see that there is no black key between the third and fourth white keys in the paper puzzle (E and F). After the puzzles are completed, the children take them back to the piano, match the black keys of the puzzle to the black keys of the piano and insert the puzzles side by side for the full length of the piano keyboard.

Fig. 14. Keyboard Puzzle

Immediately they notice that the keyboard is not an awesome immensity, but just seven white keys repeated seven times. Now they can also see that not only is there no black key between E and F, but there is also none between B and C.

At the next lesson, after the puzzle is correctly assembled, each child is asked to look at it carefully, then to close his eyes and try to see the picture of the completed puzzle in his mind's eye. Then he is asked to remove the black strips and replace them without consulting the piano. In this way the image-retention essential for sight-reading is cultivated from the beginning.

At this time, the children are not expected to learn the letter names of the notes. After frequent dramatization of the Live Keyboard, which is described below, they will gradually absorb letter names and then they can take up the Keyboard Puzzle again, this time with each *white* strip clipped into place and marked with its special name. In this way the puzzle gains fresh interest and new material for study as the children progress. When this stage of the Keyboard Puzzle has been mastered, and the completed puzzles are again placed end to end back of the piano keys, the children, standing side by side at the piano, are asked to play a note, for example the one between the two black keys (Fig. 14, bottom). By playing all the D's together, the children will hear that all their D's are related. They also discover that the low D is of a deep hue, the middle range a medium hue, and the high D a pale hue, which is a preparation for the concept of tonal color. The teacher proceeds in a like manner with as many keys as the children can absorb without becoming tired.

Clean or Messy Paintbox

While the children are exploring the sounds of notes at the piano, they can be introduced to the effect of the damper pedal. The middle child is instructed to hold the pedal down, while the rest of the children play C in the various octaves. Then the performance is repeated with all of the D's, all of the E's, and so forth. The children soon perceive that each new string of notes calls for a fresh pedal if the color of the note is to be kept clear— just as a brush must be washed between different colors of paint.

46

LIVE KEYBOARD

MATERIALS: Narrow white poster boards, each bearing the letter name of a note; narrower sheets of heavy black construction paper, marked in yellow crayon with a sharp on one side, a flat on the other.

In the Keyboard Puzzle, the children identified the piano with the different parts of the puzzle. In the Live Keyboard they identify themselves with the piano keyboard and the Keyboard Puzzle as well.

The teacher helps the children group themselves into the pattern of the keyboard. Some children will represent the white keys by holding the lettered white poster boards, and other children will represent the black keys by holding the black construction paper. If there are too few children, dolls and stuffed animals can substitute for the black keys, adding to the general fun.

Later, the children learn that the black keys do not have letter names of their own but take their names from their neighboring white keys. However, attention is not called to this fact in the beginning. The sharps and flats drawn on the black poster keys are merely in the background like furniture in a room which children may first ignore but later notice.

The first point to emphasize is that each cardboard "key" marked C, D, or E, for instance, represents a C, a D, or an E anywhere on the keyboard. Again, the objective is to familiarize the child with the keyboard and to show that there are only seven different white notes that merely repeat themselves on the piano keyboard seven times.

Even the concept of a note being "in between" two other notes is often difficult to convey to children. In the Live Keyboard game, they get, through their large muscles, a physical approach to this and many other difficult concepts. For example, the child who is D can feel C and E next to her, one on each side.

Once the children are assembled, the Keyboard Puzzle Game, which they have already played, is translated into the terms of the Live Keyboard.

Each child takes a turn running up to the piano and playing and singing "himself." The spirit of fun is kept up by a counting-off game to see which child shall have the privilege of playing and singing his key. Instead of "eeny, meeny, miney, mo," the teacher says:

> Do, re, mi,
> Strike your key.
> Mi, fa, sol,
> Reach your goal.
> La, ti, do,
> You . . . may . . . go!

Thus, for example, if she begins with the children who represent C-D-E, she touches each child as she says "Do-re-me," touching the same three again as she says "Strike your key." For "Mi-fa-sol, Reach your goal" she touches E-F-G, again twice in succession. With "La-ti-do, You may go" she touches the children who represent A-B-C, and the child she has touched on the word "go" does just that. He goes to the piano and plays and sings his note, locating his position—and the position of his note on the keyboard—by its relation, and his, to the surrounding black notes.

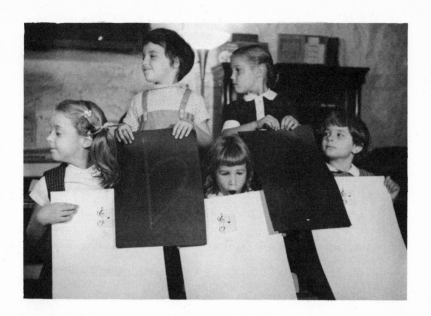

Fig. 15. Live Keyboard

"Hot Cross Buns" Come Alive

MATERIALS: *Poster board and construction paper "keys" from the Live Keyboard Game. This time, each white key has not only the letter name of the note on one side, but, on the other, a picture of that note drawn in place on the staff (Fig. 15).*

The Live Keyboard can be extended to the study of a short piece which uses three notes and a few simple time values. "Hot Cross Buns" is a familiar tune which serves the purpose well.

Hot cross buns Hot cross buns One a pen- ny Two a pen- ny Hot cross buns

The teacher begins by playing "Hot Cross Buns" on the piano. The children sing the song several times with the words; then, following the teacher, they sing the letter names of the notes in place of the words. An over-all picture of the whole piece is thus established through both hearing and singing.

Now further motor activities are added. The teacher pretends to play—indeed, she does play—the piece on the Live Keyboard, just as she played it on the piano. In time with the music, she gently presses the head of each child representing the proper note. At this the child bobs down with a rhythmic spring-action of the knees and sings the letter name of his note.

Suppose that Sally is E, Susie is D, and Babs is C. The teacher starts the first measure by pressing Sally's head. Sally sings "E" as she bobs down, her knees bending. The teacher next touches Susie, who is D, and as she does so, Susie sings "D" in pitch and also bobs once. Then the teacher presses middle-C Babs, but instead of letting her spring back as she sings "C," the teacher holds her down for an extra count, or, in other words, for the two-count value of a half note. ("Down, hold," the teacher may say in this case as she continues holding her hand over the child's head, and the child may sing "C, hold.")

The routine is repeated for the second measure, which is the same as the first. Only the second time, middle-C Babs, having

50

come up from her half-note sojourn for two counts, is bounced down four more times by the teacher for the four eighth notes, ("One-a-penny"); the same four bounces for Susie ("Two-a-penny")—"D-D-D-D" sings Susie; and again the first routine of a tap apiece for E, D, and the half-note C ("Hot Cross Buns").

The children take turns being the performers and, later, "playing" the Live Keyboard (Fig. 15, bottom). They also change their positions, thus identifying themselves with different notes. Then, like a player-piano, they act and sing out the piece, each singing and bobbing rhythmically at an exactly timed entrance into the melody.

Another piece which serves the requirements of the Live Keyboard is the "Pirate Song."

Through the identification of self with the individual keys, the development of precision-timed entrances, and the quick hearing-and-singing responses, the children and the keyboard become one.

After a few weeks, the teacher can call the names of the keys and thus command a terminology without which it is impossible to make progress on the piano or any other instrument. This terminology is now understood by the children because it has a physical reality for them which has been developed by the Live Keyboard game. Names of piano keys are names of friends, not of strangers or abstractions.

STAFF PUZZLE

MATERIALS: *Sixteen or more strips of wood 14″ long, ½″ wide, and ½″ thick, ten of them painted black for the ten black lines of the staff, and six or more painted white with a short black line on the under side for the leger lines; six strips of wood 14″ long, 1⅜″ wide, and ½″ thick, painted white for all the spaces of the staff, including the two white spaces on either side of middle C; black paper cutout clefs to superimpose on the completed staff.*

The Staff Puzzle serves in various ways as a transition—from the larger to the smaller staff, from the written staff to the sound of the corresponding notes, and from the staff to the piano keyboard.

The first time it is introduced, the disassembled line and space pieces, and one white leger-line piece for middle C, are laid on the floor beside the Floor Staff. A child is encouraged to assemble the staff, starting with the bottom line (Fig 16). As he sets each piece of wood into place, the teacher or another pupil plays the corresponding note on the piano.

Fig. 16. Staff Puzzle

The following week, the puzzle is worked on a small table beside the piano. The staff is assembled at right angles to the piano, so that the lines and spaces are end to end with the piano keys. If the dimensions of the puzzle have been properly followed, when the G-strip of the bass staff is placed opposite the corresponding note on the piano, every other line and space will fall into place opposite its appropriate note. Again, each child is given a turn to build the staff. As the child puts down each strip, another plays the note that corresponds, and the whole group sings it in a convenient register. Or better still, before putting the strip into place, the child lightly touches the strip to the right key and makes the sound himself (Fig. 17).

An advanced group can profit from having the Staff Puzzle extended to include the additional leger-line strips above and below the staff. This advanced version of the puzzle should also be used at the piano.

Fig. 17. Staff Puzzle and Singing Staff at the Piano

SINGING-STAFF MUSIC

The two pieces that follow are simple enough for beginners to learn at the piano. Since they use only the lines of the staff, they can be worked in a variety of ways with the Singing Staff and other staff games.

"Bullfrog Piece"

MATERIALS: *Singing Staff; Floor Staff; Staff Puzzle; toy bullfrog.*

The "Bullfrog Piece" uses only notes on the lines of the bass staff. It should be played by the children with one finger, to keep their attention away from fingering and to center it on the fact that consecutive lines on the staff represent a skip on the keys.

While the teacher or a child plays the "Bullfrog Piece" on the Singing Staff, each of the group takes a turn learning it at the piano. Meanwhile, another child can follow on the assembled Staff Puzzle near the piano, using a toy bullfrog to "play" the notes. The piece can also be jumped on the Floor Staff, with the jumping child pretending that he is a bullfrog. The whole group sings the notes an octave above the piano.

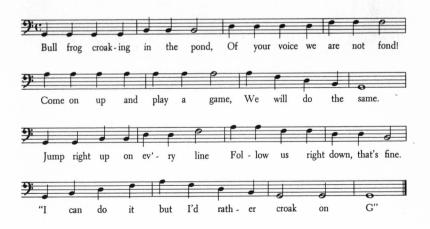

"Totem Pole Piece"

MATERIALS: Singing Staff; white paper; colored crayons.

In preparation, the children make Totem Pole staves, drawing a large staff and sketching a different face on each line in chord formation. The faces are drawn in bright colors to resemble a totem pole, and the letter name of each "Indian chief" can easily be worked into the war paint on his face. This is an introduction to the appearance of chords.

The "Totem Pole Piece" uses only notes on the lines of the treble staff. One child plays it on the Singing Staff, as another learns to play it on the piano. The tom-tom accompaniment can be described as a chorus of drummers, with one or two children in turn playing the chords on the piano and whispering "Hear those tom-toms" or some similar four-syllable phrase.

This piece provides an excellent opportunity for the development of Crescendo and Diminuendo, starting softly and working to a feverish pitch of excitement at the lines, "Masks that stare, etc." The tempo must remain steady—and the tom-toms can help to keep it so—bringing out the principle that one need not get faster as one gets louder. The piece dies away in a whisper.

CLAP-TOUCH

Clap-touch is a method for teaching time values and the relationships between the various time values—articulated and silent—in any given tempo. It must be done rhythmically, and it should always be done with singing, for it is also an exercise in coordination (Figs. 18 and 19).

Clapping out rhythms, in its most elemental form, is a familiar technique in schools. It has been developed, however, to a high point of refinement and elaboration in India where, for centuries, children have been taught to perform infinitely elaborate rhythmic patterns with a combination of hands and fingers. Clap-touch is an offshoot of this ancient teaching device.

The whole Clap-touch language is described here. However, it is up to the individual teacher to judge when the children are ready to progress beyond the simplest combinations of whole, half, quarter, and eighth notes.

Fig. 18. Clap-touch

A single hand-clap is used to indicate the basic unit of the articulated quarter note. To signify the silent beat in sustained note values—such as half notes, dotted halves, whole notes, and so fourth—the "touch" is used. This is accomplished by silently touching the back of the right hand to the palm of the left. Thus a half note is indicated by a clap and a touch, the dotted half becomes clap-touch-touch, and the whole note is clap-touch-touch-touch.

The fingers are used in Clap-touch to indicate smaller units. For articulated eighth notes, the index finger of the right hand rhythmically taps successive fingers of the left hand, held palm upward, as it is throughout clap-touch. For two eighth notes, the right index finger taps in succession the index and middle fingers of the left hand (Fig. 19, top); for three triplet eighths, the right index finger taps the index, middle, and fourth fingers of the left hand; for a group of four sixteenths, four fingers are tapped in sequence. In every case, the index finger, which is the symbol of one count, does the rhythmic tapping, and it always taps out the equivalent of a full quarter note. In this way, the relationship between the quarter note, on the one hand, and eighths, triplet eighths and sixteenths, on the other, is demonstrated in space as well as in time. (The time values represented by the fingers of the left hand of necessity vary according to the portion of a quarter note for which they must stand in any given beat.)

The back of the index finger is used to indicate silent fractions of a beat in the same way that the back of the hand is used to indicate silent beats. Thus a dotted quarter note followed by an eighth would be indicated by a clap for the quarter, a touch of the back of the index finger right hand to the front of the index finger left hand for the eighth-note dot, and a tap of the front of the right index finger to the middle finger left hand for the final eighth. Or, in Clap-touch language, clap-touch-tap (Fig. 19, center).

To clap-touch a dotted eighth note followed by an articulated sixteenth, each finger of the left hand is thought of as representing one sixteenth. Beginning with the regular tap of the right index finger on the index finger left hand (the articulated half of the eighth note), the right index finger next slides over the third and fourth fingers left hand (the silent second half of the eighth note and the dot which is the equivalent of another sixteenth); for the final articulated sixteenth, the right index finger taps the fifth finger left hand. Or, in Clap-touch language, tap-slide-slide-tap (Fig. 19, bottom).

Once the most elementary portion of Clap-touch is understood, it can be combined with walking for quarter notes, running for eighth notes, stepping then bowing for the two counts of a half note, stepping then bowing twice for a dotted half note, and stepping then bowing three times for a whole note. Clap-touch should also be combined with other rhythm games. For example, while some of the children are playing the Grandfather Clock Game, another group should clap-touch in time to the "pendulums." The various metronome games can also be clap-touched with good effect.

A step toward further rhythmic coordination is to form a clapping band, in which some children are quarter notes, some eighth notes, and others half notes. At first, a simple tune that has some of each of these time values is played, each division clapping only for its own note value. This is a valuable preparation for precisely timed entrances. Next, the teacher should play a few measures with quarter notes in one hand and eighths in the other, while the corresponding clappers perform simultaneously. All of the different time values can gradually be worked into this scheme.

Fig. 19. Clap-touch Language:

Tap-tap

Clap-touch-tap

Tap-slide-slide-tap

MEASURE POCKETS

MATERIALS: For each child, four differently colored strips of construction paper, 9" x 6", and a poster-board holder, 14" x 11". The holder is made by cutting four 9" slits, one above the other, 2" apart, in one piece of poster board. This sheet is then pasted at the edges to another poster board of equal size. The slits form pockets to hold the colored paper inserts.

The Measure Pockets are a simple device for conveying the way in which the various time values can be combined to make up a measure and a phrase. The children already know the appearance of whole notes, half notes, and quarter notes from the Treasure Hunt Game, and have begun to understand the relations between the various time values from Clap-touch. They should be introduced to the Measure Pockets by a demonstration of the relation between the parts and the whole, using something with which they are already familiar: a walnut, for instance, which can be divided into halves and again into quarters, the two halves and the four quarters adding up to a single whole; or containers of milk in quarts, pints, and half pints; or a whole tangerine and its segments.

The strips of the Measure Pockets are drawn and folded during a number of sessions (Fig. 20, top), stretching over weeks, and the activity is always accompanied by questions concerning the number of folds there are in a given strip, how many quarters there are in a half, and so forth.

To begin, each child is shown how to hold one of his strips of paper horizontally and to fold it in half from top to bottom and then to fold it again in half, thus making three parallel creases and four equal sections. The child is next asked to open the paper and to draw a whole note in the first space at the left of the strip. He now inserts this strip in the top pocket.

Next, he folds a second strip in half and cuts it on the fold, exchanging one of these two parts with a neighbor who has a paper of a different color. Now the child folds each of these two colored halves in half and draws a half note in the first space at

Fig. 20. Measure Pockets

the left of each. He then proceeds to insert these two halves side by side in the second slot. The child can readily see that the two differently colored half-note strips are equal in length to the whole-note strip above.

A third strip is folded into four parts, but now only the last fold is cut off. In the left space of the three-spaced strip that remains, a dotted half note is drawn, and again, to make the divisions more vivid, the child exchanges his quarter of the strip for one of a different color and then draws a quarter note on the new piece. The dotted half and the quarter are inserted into the third slot.

The child folds the last strip into four parts, cuts it on each of the folds, and exchanges two of his four pieces with his neighbor. Quarter notes are drawn on each of the four pieces of paper. The child inserts these pieces in the last slot, alternating the colors.

While the children are going through this procedure, the teacher demonstrates the Clap-touch values of the notes. At the next lesson, the children are asked to rearrange the note values in any way they wish, but there can be neither more nor less than four counts in each measure.

Since it is desirable to keep the common four-measure phrase intact, no extra slits are made for eighth notes. Instead, many lessons after those described above, extra strips of colored paper can be taken to represent eighth notes and inserted into any of the four existing pockets, replacing the equivalent note values already there. To do this, a strip is first folded as it was for the quarter notes and then each section is folded again. With the teacher's help, two connected eighth notes are written into each quarter of the strip, taking care that one eighth note falls into each eighth section. The uncut fold is sufficient to transmit the idea of the eighth-note length to the child.

On half-note strips, each of whose sections is folded into four units, four connected eighth notes are written. A full strip can also be cut into eight parts and a single eighth note drawn on each part.

The children can rearrange all the notes (quarters, halves,

dotted halves, wholes, and eighths) always keeping to the four-beat measure. The four measures are considered together as a phrase. In later sessions, four of these complete Measure Pocket cards, with their different arrangements of notes, can be taken together as a sixteen-measure period. They can be used to show the similarity between a musical phrase and a line of a poem, between a musical period and a stanza.

When the children are ready to study rests, the note value's corresponding rest is drawn on its reverse side and these are interspersed with the notes in the slots of the Measure Pocket (Fig. 20, bottom).

These arrangements are to be interpreted not only with singing and clapping devices, but with walking, running, and stepping with variations, with the Doodle Language (see page 93), and combinations of all of these. In every case, these coordinations should alternate with turns at the piano. There the children should play the pattern of a whole measure on one note only; later this measure can be repeated four times for a four-measure phrase feeling.

This is a good time to introduce small-sized violins and cellos. The children will need some help at first in holding and using the bow, but they will soon find that it is only a step from their rhythmic stepping, clapping, and singing to rhythmic bowings on one open string. The instrumental interpretation of the rhythmic patterns that they have created themselves makes a deep impression on the children and has resulted in more than one recruit for the string section.

Note Store

MATERIALS: Paper-money quarters with a quarter note drawn on each "coin"; paper strips marked with note values, such as those used for the Measure Pockets, or black paper cutout notes.

The children are given a store of paper-money quarters and a variety of paper notes. Then they proceed to buy and sell the notes.

64

"Big bargains in eighth notes, two for a quarter; triplets, three for a quarter; four of the fanciest sixteenth notes you've ever seen, very cheap, four for a quarter."

"Sorry, madam, but these beautiful dotted half notes will cost you three quarters. And I couldn't possibly let these lovely whole notes go for less than four quarters. Well, I might consider trading this whole note for four of your eighth notes, but you'll have to throw in that very fine half note." And so on. . . .

Grocery Bag Game

MATERIALS: *A series of measures drawn on slips of paper 2" wide and about 4" deep, with notes written out across the top in different meters and in a variety of melodic patterns; "marketing bags," made of large grocery bags turned sidewise, with four 2" slits cut end to end across the face of each, and with each bag marked with a different time signature—3/4, 2/4, 4/4, and others if the class has progressed beyond these; paper-money quarters.*

The shoppers go to a "supermarket," each one with his "marketing bag." On a large table in the "supermarket" is a display of measures for sale. The shoppers purchase enough for a four-measure phrase in the meter indicated on their bags, and slip the purchased phrases into the slits provided for them. Two children act as checker and cashier, and measures must be paid for in quarter-note coins.

Later on, when the children have begun to read music, they can also "buy" their phrases by playing them first on the piano on one note.

Sandwich Bag Game

MATERIALS: Transparent sandwich bags, each one drawn with a single note on a staff; Note Flash Cards also drawn with a note on a staff, four cards for each note; a Keyboard Chart, obtainable from music supply stores (this is a cardboard reproduction of the keyboard, in scale, which can be set upright behind the piano keys).

The children sit around a table, and each one selects a sandwich bag from a pile in the center. The teacher or one of the pupils flashes a card, and any child can claim it if it matches the note on his bag. Before he can put it into his bag, however, he must first play it on the piano. To do this, he finds his note on the Keyboard Chart that is mounted behind the keys, then plays the corresponding note beneath it. The child who first fills his bag with four matching notes wins the game.

SCALE CHARTS

MATERIALS: Colored crayons; white paper 2" wide and at least 7½" long; Cone-Royt Scale Charts. These can be approximated by cutting keyboard charts into octave lengths, one for each major scale, and on each one affixing diamond or circle cutouts to the notes appropriate to that scale. An additional chromatic chart, extending from middle C to an octave above, should have two rows of diamonds in two different colors, marked with the letter names of the notes, the top row for sharps, the bottom row for flats.

Before beginning with the Scale Charts, the teacher gathers the children around the upright piano with the cover removed. She reviews with them their trip on the Good Ship Keyboard, when they learned that the black and white keys looked the same inside the piano. Then she places the Chromatic Scale Chart behind the keys, and lays a strip of white paper along the front half of the keyboard. She plays the chromatic scale on the back of the keys, spelling it out as she goes: C-C♯-D-D♯-E-F-F♯-G-G♯-A-A♯-B-C for the ascending scale, C-B-B♭-A-A♭-G-G♭-F-E-E♭-D-D♭-C for the descending scale. The children are not expected to learn the alternate sharp and flat names of the black keys at this time, but they can be made aware that the black keys are related to the white keys and take their names from them.

The teacher now asks the children to play and to count all the keys from C to C and while so doing to notice the pattern of the felt hammers. After this she replaces the Chromatic Scale Chart with the C-major Scale Chart and removes the paper mask from the keyboard. She plays the scale and holds down all the keys while the children examine the pattern formed by the white felt hammers. Again she asks them how many notes there are, and how many notes of the first (chromatic) scale are missing. Then she plays more major scales, so that they can see that the pattern inside the piano is the same each time. Under the teacher's guidance, the children now build the scale patterns themselves, using four fingers of each hand and again holding

67

Fig. 21. Scale Charts

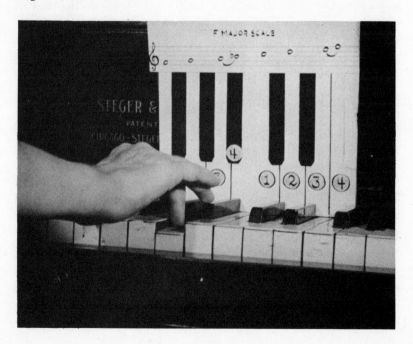

down the keys so that they can see the two half steps as they appear in the adjacent hammers (Fig. 21, top).

The background is now established for the children to use the Scale Charts, designed to give them a general concept of tonality within their first few lessons. The children seat themselves around the table and three or four charts are dealt out to each one. The children then color the diamonds on the keys, using one color for each scale. The teacher may have to color the charts for some of them.

Next, using the charts on the table as if they were keyboards, the children "play" the scale, touching the colored spots with one finger. (One little girl learned all of her scales this way when she was sick in bed.) As they finger up the scale and then down again, the teacher sings:

> Do-re-mi-fa-sol-la-ti-do,
> Do-ti-la-sol-fa-mi-re-do.

The children sing along with her as soon as they can.

The next week the charts are taken to the piano and placed upright directly behind the keyboard. The children are asked to try to match the black keys of the charts to the black keys of the piano. In some of the keys they may need some help. Now they play from the Scale Charts, following the diamonds as guides. They begin in the key of C and progress through the major scales in chromatic order. The younger ones again play the entire scale with only one finger. (The teacher need not be apologetic about the one-finger approach, since it is the basis of advanced technique for playing octaves and other large intervals in sequence.) For the older children appropriate fingering can be written into the diamonds (or, as in Fig. 21, bottom, the circles) and followed in playing, if this effort does not distract them from the central concern at this stage, which is to become acquainted with the tonalities.

Three children at a time can stand without crowding at the piano; each one puts his chart behind a different octave. Using charts of the same scale, they can then play successively or together. If there are two pianos, the teacher can play a duet part at the other instrument. She can also accompany at the lower part of the same piano, if only one child is playing.

In a few lessons, the child will have played through all of the major scales, will perceive the twelve tonalities, will know that the black keys are as important as the white, will develop a kinesthetic sense of the keyboard itself, and will not express hesitancy when later assigned music in the difficult keys. Minor scales are studied in the same manner.

When the children are ready, many lessons later, the teacher can use the backs of the charts to indicate the enharmonic key signatures and the left-hand fingering for the various scales.*

* Teachers will also find the Scale Charts useful for building the Circle of Fifths; and two sets of cards can form the basis for transposition exercises and chord studies. These subjects are treated in the authors' *A Child's Introduction to Harmony* which is now in preparation.

FIVE-FINGER WALTZ DUETS

MATERIALS: Scale Charts. The full charts already described can be used, but for clarity it is preferable to use charts with diamonds marking only the first five notes of each scale.

"Games are all very well," the conservative may well say, "but how will the child acquire the technical equipment to play an instrument if his music class is nothing but games?" Technical equipment is indeed indispensable, and for the advanced instrumentalist there is no substitute for the daily practice session on scales, arpeggios, and so forth. But these too can be pleasurable pursuits instead of grim necessities if the child has been properly introduced to them and has been physically as well as psychologically prepared to cope with them. Learning scales while the fingers are still too weak to manage them well has discouraged many a young music student. Many more have been bored by the fact that scales were presented to them as abstractions without direct musical application.

The Finger Games were designed to strengthen small fingers, to establish the proper hand position and the necessary combination of firmness and relaxation in the fingers, wrists, arms, and back. The Five-finger Waltz Duets are devised to present the old indispensable five-finger exercises in a form that will entertain the child even while he is practicing these otherwise boring musical chores.

Using the Scale Charts, one child at a time plays the first five notes of a scale up and down again, three times in all. Meanwhile, the teacher or an older pupil plays an accompaniment in waltz time, using different harmonies for each repetition. In the key of C, for example, a Five-finger Waltz Duet might sound like the music on the following page:

71

The variety of the accompaniment permits a rich harmonic pattern to infiltrate the ear of the child, suggests the many harmonic possibilities inherent in each note, and sustains the interest of the child so that he does not feel he is done at the end of the first complete pattern. The first time through, he should be given the opportunity to find the notes by watching the keyboard; the second and third times he should play without watching his fingers. It is important that each child should have an opportunity to take his five fingers through all the keys to prevent the formation of mental blocks about "difficult" keys and to give the child a kinesthetic sense of the "hills and dales" of the keyboard.

Young children like to sing words as they play. It is always best if they make up their own words, but until they are free in their playing of all the keys, they can begin with the following:

On our farms we grow po-ta-toes,
Cab-ba-ges and red to-ma-toes,
Ra-dish-es, and wa-ter-mel-ons too.

72

For older children who have acquired sufficient experience in the waltz duets, the tempo can be altered to 2/4 time. The five-finger exercise can also be played with two hands, the left hand playing *staccato* while the right hand plays *legato*, reversing the procedure halfway through the exercise. Next the left hand can play *pianissimo* while the right hand plays *forte*, again reversing the procedure midway. Another variation sets two notes in one hand against one note in the other, as well as three notes against one:

A trill exercise is developed in the following manner, first with one hand alone, then with both hands playing the same pattern:

Along with the trill exercise, the child may sing,

> Partner, partner, dance a measure.
> Partner, partner, it's a pleasure.

One child suggested this alternative:

> Partner, partner, pleased to meet you.
> Partner, partner, pleased to eat you.

Cannibalistic, but she had the rhythmic idea.

The Five-finger Waltz Duets can also be played in the minor keys, to acquaint the children with the character of the minor and to introduce new finger patterns. In fact, the possible variations are innumerable.*

* The Five-finger Waltz Duets for all keys are separately published, along with additional suggestions for their use. They can be obtained by writing Cone-Royt, care of Harper & Brothers.

Exploring the Jungle

This is a good warm-up for the Five-finger Waltz Duets. The children Explore the Jungle. The black keys are cliffs; the white keys valleys. The children pretend that they are feeling their way back into the jungle at night-fall; each finger is a member of the exploring party. They play the first five notes of each Scale Chart with their five fingers, holding all the notes down together and then rubbing their fingers from the outer edge to the inside of the keys and back, many times, without looking at their hands or the keyboard. In this way they develop a feeling for the relations and distances between the black keys and the white in each five-note scale pattern.

One child described the process as "putting my fingers into my C-major [or D-major, and so forth] gloves."

74

INTERVALS

MATERIALS: Floor Staff.

On the immediate recognition of interval relationships—visual, aural, and manual—depends a great part of sight-reading technique. This study of intervals is planned to develop an instantaneous discrimination between adjacent notes—which are seconds—and larger intervals.

It begins—literally at the bottom—on the Floor Staff. The teacher plays two notes in succession on the piano. Then the children demonstrate the interval on the Floor Staff. If the notes are adjacent, they step from one to the other, singing the interval as they go. If the notes are not adjacent, that is, not line-to-adjacent-space or space-to-adjacent-line, they jump from one to the other (Fig. 22).

Fig. 22. Jumping Intervals

When the group is studying an elementary piece, they step and jump it on the Floor Staff, analyzing the relationship of each note to its neighbor, always singing as they go.

Soon they are ready to concentrate on specific intervals in more detail. For example, if "fourths" are the subject of study, the children begin by stepping on the Floor Staff, while singing to piano accompaniment, the scale-like progression GABC, and then stepping backward and singing CBAG. Next they sing the interval of the fourth, jumping from G to C and then jumping backward from C to G. Now each child goes to the piano and performs the same upward and downward movement with his fingers, first stepping GABC, CBAG, then jumping GC and CG. This direct transference of the floor action to the keyboard must again be accompanied by singing—first from written-out patterns which the teacher has placed on the rack and then with the eyes closed. The process is then repeated all the way up the staff. On other occasions other intervals are used in the same way.

Game of Leaps

The Game of Leaps is played by each child in turn at the piano. The children choose a fairly low note in the bass as a home base, and that note is played with the left little finger (in later variations, the home base note can be played by the fourth, third, second, or first finger).

If G is chosen as a home base, the first goal is a half step ahead (G-sharp). The child says, "Leap." On the first consonant, "l," the little finger strikes the key; as the last consonant, "p," is reached, the release of the first key becomes one with the landing on the second. However—and this is important—the goal note is not played; the finger merely *lands* on it. The release of the home-base note and the silent landing on the goal is one reflex-speed movement. *No wrong notes are ever played.* The morale-building value of this is inestimable.

If the landing has been successful, the child again cries, "Leap," and jumps back in one reflex movement, from the goal note to

76

home base, again striking only the first of the two notes. If the first landing was not successful, the child gets two more chances.

The next goal is always a note a half step higher than the last. Each child is allowed three errors before he is "out." The next child then takes his turn. The winning goal is a tenth away from home base.

Large, staved cards, showing just the two notes of each leap should be made by the teacher and placed on the rack, one at a time, to correspond with the instrumental "leap." In time, the children sing the word "leap" in the pitch of the key they are about to strike. In this way, the manual measurement is coordinated with the visual and the aural.

This practice is an important step toward a kinesthetic sense of the keyboard, working toward the ability to play without looking at the keys. Let the child feel distances away from his own center. If he is sitting directly in front of the center of the instrument (which is not middle C but the crack between E and F), he will soon feel the measurement in both directions from the center of himself and the keyboard. Children enjoy practicing jumps on the piano while their eyes are closed, and from the purely technical standpoint, the "touch system" is the *sine qua non* of sight-reading.

If there are any string students in the group, they can carry over the same process to their individual instruments.

SCROLL READING

MATERIALS: Musical Scrolls made by drawing staves on shelf paper, 17" long and 7" wide. Beginning at the end, the paper is folded over a half inch, then over again, another half inch, until it is wound as tightly as possible with sixteen half-inch folds. Enough space remains to write in the clefs and time signatures. On each scroll a four-measure piece is copied, allowing for one quarter-note value between each fold. After a half note, there will be one empty fold, after a whole note, three. Next the end of the scroll is pasted to a strip of wood ¼" wide and 12" long, then wound up and fastened with a rubber band.

Several Musical Scrolls, with a different four-measure piece on each, are placed in a jar on top of the piano. The teacher picks out the easiest one and slowly unfurls it for a child seated at the piano. As she unrolls it, count by count, she asks, "Is it going up?" "Is it going down?" "Is it stepping or skipping?" The children enjoy watching these note "movies" and are full of curiosity to see what the next note will do.

Soon they begin to play the notes they see (Fig. 23), and enjoy picking out their own pieces from the jar on the piano. It should be remembered that this game is meant as their first experience in reading and its practical use is limited to simple four- or eight-measure phrases without eighth notes. The first pieces should be for one hand only, but both staves must always be present, so that a single simultaneous image of the treble and bass staves together approximates one word in a horizontal reading line. When the child is about to tackle his first piece for two hands together, Scroll Reading is again helpful.

The Scroll can also be used in combination with the Live Keyboard, with the group "playing" the piece on the Live Keyboard as one child or the teacher unfurls the Scroll in tempo.

Developed for left-to-right reading, the Scroll directs the field of vision, and the child's focus is intensified. The allocation of one quarter-note value to each fold (with an empty fold after a half note) provides a demonstration of time values in space as well as in time. In the size and simplicity of its elements, the Scroll avoids the frustration that a child feels when he first examines the fine printing of musical scores, with all the additional pedagogical detail which usually crowds music primers. Since the teacher holds the Scroll at the child's eye level, this also avoids the strain that a small child experiences when looking up at the music rack.

By removing all the distractions, and by bringing the music to the child's own level, both physical and intellectual, the Scroll gives him a happy initiation into music reading, and an easy opportunity for pure concentration.

Fig. 23. Scroll Reading

Window-shade Chords

MATERIALS: A large Grand Staff drawn on a window shade, with a crease or a yellow line for middle C.

The teacher writes a G-major chord on the Window-shade Staff—G and D in the bass, B and D in the treble. Then, with a child at the piano, the teacher unrolls the shade slowly, while the child learns to read the chord from the bottom, an essential for the future study of harmony. In later sessions, the teacher varies the chords. The children watch the unrolling with keen expectation. "What's coming?" develops into the invaluable habit of thinking, "What chord will it be?"

MUSICAL NOTATION

Checkers

MATERIALS: A 5' length of shelf paper staff-lined with spaces the width of a yardstick; checkers.

The children are given boxes of checkers and begin by placing black checkers on the lines and red or, if possible, white checkers on the spaces of the staff, to sharpen line-and-space discrimination. Next they start to copy the pieces they are learning, or will be learning, again using red checkers for the spaces and black for the lines (Fig. 24, top). Small doses of dictation—steps and skips up and down—may also be played and sung by the teacher and "taken down" by the children as they gleefully push the checkers around.

On holidays the resourceful teacher can incorporate the holiday motif into this game by substituting the little stickers sold in the shape of hearts, pumpkins, bells, and so forth, for the movable checker notes; even black gum-drops or lollypops can be used for special occasions.

With these musical checkers the children acquire, in an easy and relaxed manner, a preparation for writing music. Moving and placing the checker piece into its proper place is easier and quicker than drawing the same note. Besides, there are no erasure problems.

The reading and writing of notes presented in this fashion is a bridge to the later small-muscle movement necessary for writing music in the music notebooks. Moreover (and most important for the future) it is done in a happy frame of mind.

Tracing-paper Music

MATERIALS: Elementary music books; tracing paper; pencils; clips or masking tape.

From the notation in checkers to tracing music through paper is a logical progression toward the necessary control for writing out music. This technique develops in a natural and easy manner, since children enjoy peering at the music through the tracing paper and find it pleasurable to trace the clefs, the symbols, and the notes that they would find impossible to copy otherwise.

In the first stage of this game, which one five-year-old girl named "Peek-a-Boo," the teacher clips or sticks tracing paper over the first pieces in the children's music study books. The paper has been lined to fit over the lines in the printed piece. All the children find keen delight in tracing the music. They never fail to work from left to right, which is convincing evidence of their complete absorption in the task.

At other times, the teacher plays a series of notes and then presents the same series written out for the children to trace. This time, however, the tracing paper is unlined. Once the children have sung and copied the notes onto the tracing paper, they lift it and move it up or down on a sheet of lined music paper without notes. The notes on the tracing paper have now been shifted to a new set of lines and spaces, and then still another. Together the teacher and pupils sing and play each new position of the melodic pattern. This is the child's first real contact with sequences, and a step preparatory to transposition.

Tracing-paper Shorthand

MATERIALS: Four-measure phrases written on music paper and covered with tracing paper; pencils.

This device can be used with children of the third-grade level as well as with older students. The child is given one of the four-measure phrases covered with tracing paper; he is asked to draw a line indicating the general movement of the notes up or down. Then the teacher places tracing paper over music that contains a variety of intervals and scale-like passages. She asks the children to draw a straight diagonal line slanting up or down to indicate the scale-like progressions. Repeated notes or held notes are indicated by a straight horizontal line. All skips are to be represented by arcs ending in an arrow that indicates the direction of the jump. This way of charting intervals on paper closely parallels the stepping and jumping of intervals on the Floor Staff (see page 90). Thus, the diagonal line on paper for a scale-like progression of notes corresponds to the stepping from note to adjacent note on the Floor Staff; and the arc that represents a skip from one note to another that is not adjacent corresponds to the jump on the Floor Staff.

In Tracing-paper Shorthand, "Yankee Doodle" would look like this:

In conjunction with this study, a series of musical phrases covered over with tracing paper are handed to the children. The tracing paper bears straight lines for repeated notes and slanted ascending or descending lines for similar progressions. The phrases are played by the teacher and the children identify their pieces according to the lines. Here is an aural as well as a visual approach.

Many of the children's early pieces should be transcribed in this manner by the children themselves. The ultimate result will be a mental flash resembling a stenographic note-pad; but it will be a flash that illuminates the measures ahead.

Construction of Sharps, Flats, Naturals

MATERIALS: *Strips of black construction paper, some cut long, some short, and some in the curve of half a heart; cut-out paper notes; Floor Staff.*

To develop the instantaneous recognition of sharps, flats, and naturals, the children construct these symbols directly on the Floor Staff, using the construction-paper strips provided for them (Fig. 24, bottom). They place these in front of cutout paper notes that have been put on various lines and spaces. They are told to be careful in "boxing in" the particular line or space they are "sharping" or "flatting," as the case may be. The naturals, too, must "box in" the line or space affected. What would be a complex drawing problem for most children becomes simple fun.

Later, all the key signatures are constructed on the Floor Staff in the same fashion. Then whenever the child begins to sight-read a piece in a key other than C, if he neglects to play a required sharp or flat, he goes to the Floor Staff. There he takes the black strips and constructs the key signature of his new piece; next he places the paper notes down on all the lines and spaces affected by the signature. He comes back to the piano with reassurance; from now on, all the F's will be sharped in the key of G.

Fig. 24. Musical Notation: top, Checkers; bottom, Construction of Sharps, Flats, and Naturals

"JUST ONE MORE" RELAY

When the children know a piece well, either from memory or from music, they are ready to play this game. The first child plays the first note and stops. The next child runs up, relay fashion, and plays the first note and "just one more"; the game continues, each child starting from the beginning and adding one more note. If the group is large enough to divide into teams, his own team whispers "Stop" whenever the player wants to do too much, to prevent his losing a point for the team. No one is dropped from the game, however; the objective is to keep everyone concentrating.

A more intricate variation of the "Just One More" Relay starts with the children gathered around the piano. They sing the note letter-names of an elementary piece of eight-measure length which they have memorized. When the last note is ready to sound, the last child in the circle around the piano plays that note. The next time around, everyone sings from the beginning once more, only this time the child next to the end plays the last two notes; and so on until the beginning is reached. This variation is only for an older group.

These games are invaluable aids to the memorization of music. Not only is a full concentration brought into play, but hidden spider-webs in the memory are cleaned out.

CELEBRATIONS

Grown-ups should encourage children to bring their music into active participation in every possible celebration. Only through a deeply personal experience can the functional use of music be grasped by the child.

After a few months of piano study, the "Happy Birthday Song" can generally be taught to a child of seven or eight. With this in his repertory, he is equipped to regale his friends and relatives perennially.

If this tune is presented in the key of G, violin and cello beginners can reinforce the melody line, or join the young pianist with suitable open strings for accompaniment.

It is wise to start teaching the Christmas Carols in the fall. Since the children are bursting with anticipation anyhow, once the excitement of Halloween and Thanksgiving is over, it is only good horse sense to harness some of this energy to pull the old music lessons out of their rut.

Holiday Lyrics

The pieces in most piano books contain lyrics or words under the notes; but by composing his own words, the child can gain a special feeling for the strong and weak beats of the rhythm, for the time values and rhythmic divisions in general, and for the complete phrase. Even simple pieces that can be taught at almost the first lesson can be adapted to fit the holiday spirit. For example, the following sets of words were composed by children to the music of "Hot Cross Buns" (see page 50). In the search for syllables that fit, the original quarter notes were divided into eighths in all but the birthday version, and provided an invaluable lesson in strong and weak beats, time values, and, above all, in phrasing.

Hal-low-een is here, Hal-low-een is here,
We are danc-ing, We are pranc-ing,
Hal-low-een is here.

. . .

Bless Thanksgiving Day, Bless Thanksgiving Day,
First we meet, and then we eat, oh,
Bless Thanksgiving Day.

. . .

Holidays are here, Holidays are here,
Bells are ringing, Bells are singing,
Holidays are here.

. . .

Birthday Child, Birthday Child,
We've been told, he's eight years old, oh,
Birthday Child.

SIGHT-READING GAMES

The constant awareness of ascending and descending lines is of utmost importance in sight-reading facility. With this must be integrated the instant, reflex-action differentiation between intervals. Through the early flash-card games and others such as Schumann Says, the children have begun to develop an instantaneous response to musical stimuli; with the preparation of the Garden Seeds Game, and later with Scroll Reading, they have begun to perceive upward and downward movement; and with the interval games and tracing-paper graphs, they have learned not only to differentiate between adjacent notes and larger intervals, but also to characterize them as rising or descending intervals. The next step is the development of image retention.

Image Retention Game

MATERIALS: *Note Flash Cards.*

A child holds a flash card up for all the others to see. Then the teacher flashes other cards one at a time for an instant only. The children instantly describe each note as higher or lower than the original one. In subsequent versions of this game, the children are asked to find the note on the staff and the keyboard.

Fig. 25. Interval Charades

Interval Charades

MATERIALS: *Floor Staff; Two-red-line Flash Cards, with the staff drawn in black, except for two lines—different ones on each card—which are drawn in red.*

These twisters, and the ones that follow, are for that older group that sometimes says, "Aw, that's too easy!"

A card is flashed, and the children immediately straddle the two indicated lines on the Floor Staff. When they have mastered this, they add the appropriate Body Staff motions. For example, if the Flash Card has the bottom two lines of the bass staff in red, each child will have his left foot on G, with his left hand touching that foot; his right foot will be on the B-line, with his right hand touching his right knee (Fig. 25). At the same time, he sings the notes he stands on.

The game can be varied by including the spaces: the child is asked to run to the space *between* the red lines, or adjacent to the top or bottom red line. This can also be turned into a charade game in which the children guess what is being acted out on the Floor Staff and play the answers on the piano.

Interval Sign Language

This is useful when a quiet moment is desired. The intervals up to fifths are expressed by the fingers, assuming the same position they would if they were playing the interval on the piano: thumb and second finger for a second; thumb and third finger for a third, and so forth. This can be done in response to interval flash cards, interval playing on the piano, or in connection with Interval Hopscotch (see below).

Interval Hopscotch

MATERIALS: *Floor Staff; a cardboard sheet, 18" x 24", with a staff drawn on it, the lines an inch apart; several sheets of tracing paper to fit, each with two notes written on it in such a way that when the paper is laid over the cardboard staff it will mark an interval of a second, a third, a fourth, or a fifth.*

One child chooses a tracing-paper interval and places it on the cardboard staff so that the bottom note is superimposed on the bottom line of the staff. Then the rest of the group straddles the interval on the Floor Staff. The child moves the tracing paper gradually up the cardboard staff, and the group jumps up the Floor Staff to match.

This gives the children the "look" of the interval. Another child stands at the piano, playing the appropriate notes, to give them the "sound." When these coordinations are well in hand, they add the Interval Sign Language, to give the "feel" (Fig. 26).

Fig. 26. Interval Hopscotch with Sign Language

Hopscotch of Intervals with Partners

This variation of Interval Hopscotch helps to familiarize children with the all-important interval of the sixth. The materials are the same, except that the tracing-paper interval is now a sixth. While one child moves the tracing paper up the cardboard staff, and another plays it on the piano, a pair of children, acting as partners, jump the interval up the floor staff.

Hopscotch of Intervals in Sequence

MATERIALS: Cardboard staff used in Interval Hopscotch; three tracing paper strips to fit, each with one of the following sequences of intervals drawn on it: third, second, third, fourth, third; third, fourth, fifth, fourth, third; third, second, third, fourth, fifth; in each sequence of intervals the bottom note remains the same.

This version of Interval Hopscotch resembles more closely the original children's game. One child holds a tracing paper sequence over the cardboard staff, with the bottom note of the first interval on the bottom line. Another child plays the intervals in sequence on the piano, while the remainder of the group jump them on the Floor Staff. This series is repeated up the whole staff. The game is then varied by using another tracing paper sequence of intervals.

These interval sequences are first done in C-major, but later they can be jumped and played in various keys.

92

DOODLE LANGUAGE

The Doodle Language sounds downright silly, but is actually an advanced study in rhythmic control and articulation.

The skilled practitioners of the musical arts of India initiate children into the most elaborate rhythms for their Temple ritual music by means of nonsense syllables. A distinguished pianist, who learned and performed twenty-four Mozart concerti in a few months, confided that in order to remember which runs came in which concerto, she had to "doodle doodle" and "doodle-dee-doodle" mentally all the way through. Here is the Doodle Language slightly simplified for beginners.

"Doo" is the quarter note. ♩

A slightly separate "oo" is added in as smooth a manner as possible for every quarter-note value contained in any note sustained for more than one beat. Thus:

"Doo-oo" is the half note. ♩

"Doo-oo-oo" is the dotted half note. ♩.

"Doo-oo-oo-oo" is the whole note. ○

New syllables are added for units of eighths and sixteenths. Thus:

"Doo-dull" is two successive eighth notes. ♫

"Doo-dull-dee" is three triplet eighth notes. ♫♩

"Doo-dull-loo-dull" is four sixteenths. ♬♬

"Doo-dull-lee, loo-dull-lee" is a group of six sixteenths, subdivided into two groups, together equal to one quarter note.

"Doo-dull, loo-dull, loo-dull" is a group of six sixteenths, subdivided into three groups.

93

A group of eight thirty-second notes, worth one quarter note, is:
"Doo-dull-loo-dull, loo-dull-loo-dull"

A group of twelve to a single count:
"Doo-dull-loo-dull, loo-dull-loo-dull, loo-dull-loo-dull"

Note that the "doo" syllable which stands for a quarter note comes *only* at the beginning of each unit and does not recur until the following quarter-note beat. The numbers "one," "two," "three," and so forth, may later be substituted at the beginning of each quarter-note unit, beginning with "one" at each new measure.

Any syllables could have been used, but these have the following advantages; they can be rolled off at tremendous speed, they can be done invisibly with the mouth closed, and they can be articulated inaudibly so as not to interfere with the simultaneous playing of an instrument. This can be demonstrated with the Largo Movement of Beethoven's D-major Trio* where the quarter note is divided into three, four, six, eight, twelve, and other divisions.

A child of ten can learn this syllabification of music and will find it infinitely helpful throughout his musical career, professional or amateur.

* Op. 70. No. 1, measures 15–20.

OLD-FASHIONED SEWING MACHINE

The original Grandfather Clock Game with its broad, swinging pendulum movements that expressed the pulse of the accompanying music is now compressed into a new game that has the same purpose. However, instead of large movements of the arm which would not be possible if one tried to play an instrument simultaneously, the child now uses small movements of the left foot to imitate the foot pedal of an old-fashioned sewing machine. This can be mastered so that it can be done with almost invisible movements by the left toe within the shoe. Furthermore, this activity can be carried on while one is playing any instrument.

Except in instances of special effect, the down-beat of the foot is the strong beat of the 2/4 or 4/4 measure and the up-beat of the foot is the weak beat, approximating the scanning of poetry. In 4/4 meter, the foot would go down on "one," up for "two," down for "three," and up for the weak beat of "four." For 3/4 or other triple division, the foot goes down slightly to the left, makes a slight slide along the floor to the right, and comes up with a strong up-beat on the count of three, describing a small triangle, as the arm did in the early conducting games. Beginners usually hesitate at the last beat in a measure; but once they have done this down-beat and up-beat foot-pedal study, they realize that what goes up must come down, and so they move unhesitatingly from one measure to the next.

Once the child can get the habit of feeling the rhythm unobtrusively with the left foot, he can use this device later in his career, if he should ever find himself sight-reading rhythmically difficult chamber music. Then, too, each down and up of the foot pulse can be fitted to half measures or whole measures where counter-rhythms, polyrhythms, transitions to proportional changes of meter, and so forth, make heavier demands on the performer's rhythmic poise. Many professional string quartet players use some form of this device.

The Sewing Machine Game is especially therapeutic for children with an underdeveloped rhythmic sense.

The Doodle Language can be combined with the foot pulse and actual sight-reading, so that the Doodle syllables, the foot pulse, and the playing are all fitted into the strong and weak beats of the measure.

This calls for a truly high degree of coordination.

LEGER LINES AND THE TENOR AND ALTO CLEFS

Surveyors

MATERIALS: For each child a strip of shelf paper at least 4' long; sheets of tracing paper at least 20" long; yellow crayon; red crayon; pencils.

When a child feels thoroughly at home with the treble and bass staves, he is ready for a project that will both familiarize him with the leger lines above and below the staves and at the same time initiate him into the mysteries of the alto and tenor clefs used by the viola and 'cello.

Each child becomes a surveyor. In order to map out the keyboard, he brings his equipment—shelf paper and crayons—to the piano. He measures off a strip of the shelf paper to fit the length of the property he is surveying—the piano keyboard. Starting at the second white key at the extreme left of the piano, he draws a yellow line across the shelf paper to represent this key, and then draws a similiar line for every other white key all the way up the keyboard. The line that represents middle C is drawn in red. (Since there are 52 white keys, he will draw 26 lines, but this he should find out for himself.) The lines will be approximately 1⅞" apart (Fig. 27).

When the child looks at his completed survey, the teacher asks him, "Wouldn't it be dreadful to read music from such a sheet of music paper? Yet every line and space represents a sound that we often want to use. How can we arrange to read all these notes comfortably?"

After a few suggestions are offered, the teacher is ready to demonstrate the solution to this problem. For this purpose, every surveyor now takes some tracing paper and draws the Grand Staff of treble and bass clef with the lines the same distance apart as the yellow lines on the shelf paper, and with the invisible line of middle C indicated with a faint pencil mark. Now they superimpose the lines of this tracing paper Grand Staff on the yellow lines of the long shelf-paper sheet, being careful to match the pencilled middle-C line to the red line underneath. What a sense of relief when it suddenly becomes clear that the staff, with its lines and spaces, covers all but 15 of the yellow lines, leaving only six leger lines below and nine leger lines above. Since the staff lines are black, while the yellow leger lines show through the tracing paper only dimly, it is easy to demonstrate how these lines are invisible and only come into being when a note appears thereon. The children are already familiar with this concept from their study of middle C.

Fig. 27. Surveyors

Surveying the Clefs

MATERIALS: *4' lengths of poster board; yellow and red crayons; tracing paper; pencils.*

Once the concept of the convenience of the treble and bass clefs is thoroughly grasped, the groundwork is laid for introducing the alto and tenor clefs which are used by the viola and cello. These, too, are used for convenience, as the children will prove to themselves.

Instead of using shelf paper this time, for practical purposes the yellow lines for every other white key on the piano are drawn on a stiff piece of poster board. Again the middle-C line is painted in red. The children now make several tracing-paper staves of five lines each, the lines as far apart as the poster-board lines. On one of these a G-clef is drawn; on another an F-clef; on still another a C-clef is drawn with the point of the clef marking the middle line (the alto clef); and on a fourth, another C-clef is drawn, this time with the point of the clef marking the next to the top line (the tenor clef).

Each of these tracing-paper staves is matched in turn to the poster-board sheet (Fig. 28): the F-clef sits on the five lines below middle C; the G-clef sits on the five lines above middle C; next, the alto clef sits with its middle- or C-line superimposed on the red middle C of the poster board; the tenor clef also sits with its C-line on the poster-board C, but this time, C is the next to the top line on the tracing paper. The former "invisible" red line of C now becomes a *visible* part of the tenor or alto staff.

Imagination should run riot at this point. The children should be reminded of the Flower Staff Game which was, in fact, preparation for Surveying the Clefs. In that case, each gardener could be likened to an instrument "watering" his particular part of the entire staff. Now, perhaps, each tracing-paper staff is a prospector, staking his claim on the map the surveyors have prepared, or a farmer plotting his farmland on a different section of the country of sound. The important point is that each instrument uses a section of the entire staff that is convenient for its range and therefore demands the smallest use of the leger lines.

Cellos and violas and violins should be brought in to demonstrate the convenience of the various clefs. At this point, too, it will not be amiss to pass around pictures of the medieval staves and to tell of some of the first attempts to write music. Even the red line has a historical basis, since one of the first staves in use had one red line.

As always it is a good idea to make several presentations of the same material. Thus the Staff Puzzle with the extra leger-line pieces can be laid out directly on the poster-board "map" of the keyboard. Also, a window shade can be substituted for the poster board, again superimposing the tracing-paper clefs on the yellow lines of the shade. As a piece of equipment, the shade is practical, occupies little space, and is always accessible.

The study of leger lines and the tenor and alto clefs provides an appropriate transition to the study of the fingerboard instruments, which is sketched in Appendix D of this book.

Fig. 28. Surveying the Clefs: top, tenor clef; bottom, alto clef

APPENDICES

Fig. 29. Cone-Royt Singing Staff

APPENDIX A

DIRECTIONS FOR MAKING
CONE-ROYT SINGING STAFF

*MATERIALS: 1 wooden board, 18" high, 23½" wide, and ⅞"
thick, painted white; 20 small-sized screw-eyes; several yards of
strong hat elastic, black (Fig. 29).*

Across the exact middle of the board, draw a light horizontal
line to represent middle C.

At both outer edges of the board, draw dots an inch apart—five
above the middle-C line and five below the middle-C line. Now
draw the five lines for the treble or G staff and five lines for the
bass or F staff, using the dots for accurate spacing.

At the exact center of the bottom line of the bass staff mark a
dot.

At the exact center of the top line of the treble staff mark a
dot.

Measure and mark one dot 8" to the left and one dot 8" to the
right of the center dot on the bottom line of the bass staff.

Next, measure and mark one dot 3⅜" to the left and one dot
3⅜" to the right of the center dot on the top line of the treble
staff.

Place a yardstick connecting the left dot of the bottom line
with the left dot of the top line; mark dots along the rule on the
remaining lines, omitting the C line. Now do the same on the
right side.

Insert screw-eyes into these dots and screw them in lightly. Be
careful not to fasten the screw-eyes too tightly as it will be necessary to tighten them later to tune the elastic to the correct pitch.

Cut ten pieces of the black elastic (about 12" long). Thread
the lowest left-side screw-eye with a piece of the cut elastic. Tie

105

firmly. Then, thread the corresponding right-side screw-eye with the same piece of elastic, and pull tightly to the approximate pitch. Wind the screw-eye counterclockwise several times and tie the elastic firmly.

Thread and tie each of the remaining nine elastic "lines" to each left-side screw-eye and thread, pull, wind, and tie to its corresponding right-side screw-eye.

Take the board to the piano and tune the elastics to their proper pitch by inserting a large nail through the right-side screw-eye and turning until the correct pitch is attained. Turn right to make the pitch higher. Until the elastic "sets," the staff will have to be tuned frequently.

To finish the project, measure a margin an inch from the left of the board and connect the two staves with the customary line and bracket. Draw a treble clef on the upper staff and a bass clef on the lower staff. At the extreme right, place a double bar connecting the two staves.

The pencilled lines extending beyond the elastic "lines" and the clefs can now be painted with black enamel, using a fine brush.

An extra pair of screw-eyes with white elastic can be set in occasionally to illustrate the invisible middle-C line and the concept of the one Grand Staff formed by the treble and bass.

The Singing Staff described above is an instrument which anyone with sufficient dexterity and the necessary materials should be able to construct. A more zither-like instrument, with wire or gut strings and with an opening in the center of the sounding board to give added resonance would, of course, be preferable for the purpose, and is in preparation.

APPENDIX B

CONE-ROYT PRACTICE KEYBOARD

A mute piano or practice Klavier has always been fairly expensive and heavy to carry. The Cone-Royt Practice Keyboard uses foam rubber for the white keys and ½"-wide strips of black sponge rubber for the black keys, all cut to the pattern of the piano keys. It can be rolled up and carried anywhere (Fig. 30).

Finger exercises are seldom appreciated by those forced to listen. Just as a dancer exercises at the bar, so can a piano student exercise on this practice keyboard without disturbing anyone. But silent practice does not mean that one hears nothing—one hears with the mind. The late Moritz Rosenthal, a virtuoso pianist, was fond of saying to those who inadvertently stepped into his hotel room while he was practicing on his mute piano, "Beautiful, isn't it?"

Fig. 30. Cone-Royt Practice Keyboard

APPENDIX C

CHART OF SUGGESTED ACTIVITIES

The lists of suggested activities that follow are intended as an informal guide to a variety of ways in which the materials of this book can be combined into hour-long lessons. These lessons are not planned to follow one another in rigid sequence; rather they indicate in general terms a possible order of study, beginning with a list of pre-school materials, combining these with some slightly more complicated games for a school-aged beginners' group, and progressing gradually to increasingly difficult materials appropriate to children up to twelve years of age and advanced in musical experience. Such a series of lessons could well be spread out over a three- or four-year course, interspersed with other variations on the materials in this book, as well as with rhythm band work, eurhythmics, and other elementary musical training. At the end of such a course, those students interested in strings would be prepared for further instrumental instruction such as that for Fingerboard Training described in Appendix D.

Pre-school Activities

Treasure Hunt; Black Lines and White Squares; Bug Game; Tightrope Walk; Trucks on Highways; Boats on Rivers; Garden Seed Game; Conducting; Gingerbread Staff Children; Clef Bracelets; Finger Games; Schumann Says (Simon Says); Live Staff: concept of bottom, middle, and top; Open-string Bowing. Also such traditional activities as Rhythm Band and Rhythm Sticks to records, Marching, walking, running, etc., singing and clapping.

109

Lesson Plans

I

Treasure Hunt
Parade of the Fingers: trucks under knuckles
Garden Seed Game
Clapping and walking for quarter notes
Matching quarter notes to wall notes
Notebook Drawing: quarter notes

II .

Treasure Hunt for clefs
Clef Bracelets
Clap-touch for half notes
Dance of the Fingers: Step-Bow
Treasure Hunt for half notes
Notebook Drawing: half notes, clefs, and hands with staff
Simon Says for clef hands (Clef Bracelets are worn during game)
Simon Says for finger numbering
Tightrope Walk on Floor Staff
Review: Garden Seed Game

III

Rocking-chair Game
Lyric composing
Grandfather Clock Game (done to Rocking-chair song)
Stepping up and down Floor Staff
Live or Body Staff (concept of up and down)
Cotton Picking, Pick Up Sticks, Parade of the Fingers
Garden Seed Game

IV

Hanging On to the Boat, Parade of the Fingers
Keyboard Puzzle

Shuffleboard on Floor Staff
Gingerbread Staff Children
Conducting 2/4 and 4/4 with square frames
Grandfather Clock Game: whole notes
Treasure Hunt for whole notes
Clef Bracelets: Pipe Cleaner Game

V

Keyboard Puzzle (learn seven white keys)
Clean or Messy Paintbox
Live Keyboard
Live Keyboard playing of "Pirate Song"
Conducting and Grandfather Clock of "Pirate Song"
Dance of the Fingers

VI

The Metro-gnome
Bell Game
Measure Pockets
Beanbag Game
Five-finger Waltz Duets (hands separately)
Conducting 3/4 time with triangle frames
Checkers: line and space discrimination

VII

Clap-touch of dotted half notes
Conducting 3/4 with triangle frames as accompaniment to Five-
    finger Waltz Duets
Measure Pockets: four-measure phrase
Intervals: stepping and jumping elementary piece
Checker copying of same piece
Scroll Reading of same piece: Live Keyboard and actual piano

111

VIII

Dance of the Fingers on mats
Exploring the Jungle
Five-finger Waltz Duets
Tracing of elementary piece
Floor Staff stepping and jumping of piece
Scroll and Live Keyboard of same
Pin the Note on the Staff

IX

Parade of the Fingers
Staff Puzzle done at piano
"Bullfrog Piece"
Scale Charts at table
Sandwich Bag Game
Printing-set Staff

X

Scale Charts with demonstration of interior of piano
Measure Pockets with rests
Statues
"Totem Pole Piece"
Interval Charades
Construction of sharps, flats, and naturals

XI

Interval Hopscotch
Ear training: Interval Sign Language
One-red-line Flash Cards
Tracing-paper Shorthand of simple piece
Scale Charts
Five-finger Waltz Duets (two hands together)

XII

Measure Pockets: eighth notes
Alternation of walking and running to quarter notes and eighth
   notes
Clap-touch of eighths
Measure Pockets: four-measure-phrase patterns with bowing of
   open strings and playing of patterns on one note at the piano
Five-finger Waltz Duets with eighth note variation
One-red-line Flash Card Game on Floor Staff

XIII

Grocery Bag Game
Flower Garden Staff
Hopscotch of Intervals with Partners
Image Retention Game
Scale Charts
Group learning of piece: Scroll, Floor Staff, Tracing, Checkers,
   Clap-touch, Conducting, and Grandfather Clock

XIV

Review of dotted half note and introduction of dotted quarter:
   Clap-touch, Measure Pocket, and instrumental application of
   dotted quarters
Group learning of piece as above
New variations of Five-finger Waltz Duets: trills
Doodle Language

XV

Doodle Language in new piece
Old-fashioned Sewing Machine
Clap-touch of more advanced rhythms
Surveyors: Leger Lines
"Just One More" Relay of old piece

113

APPENDIX D

FINGERBOARD EAR-TRAINING

by Madeleine Carabo-Cone

The symphonic situation is serious. In newspapers and magazines, our leading orchestral conductors regularly deplore the shortage of string instrument students and the lack of a reservoir for future symphony orchestras. Our rich musical inheritance lies in a wealth of symphonic and chamber music masterpieces, yet within a few generations, live performances of these could well become a thing of the past.

The band instruments, which can be learned to competency within a few years, have flourished to such an extent that a leading music school had to institute a quota system to limit the number of band instrument students. Yet although the strings take many more years to master and training must therefore start early, the trend in elementary education is increasingly to postpone any fingerboard training or staff-reading until the child is "ready." This "readiness" is considered apparent at the age of eleven or thereabouts, and indeed this is an age where a child can be expected to cope with stringed instruments even with run-of-the-mill teaching. But the child of seven or eight would be equally ready for instrumental training if the presentation were at least as vivid, imaginative, and tangible as the newer methods of teaching arithmetic.

For a national revival of string instrument playing we must look to the public schools. Even in the kindergarten and the first grade the child can prepare for the study of a musical instrument by acquiring a solid foundation in rhythmic patterns and intervals, which are the two basic elements of fingerboard technique. In the body of this book we have outlined a program for primary music education through games, activities, and projects that bring the fundamentals of rhythm, ear training, sight-reading, and general musicianship close to children in a way consistent

115

with the rest of the school program. We have shown how the child's own construction of Measure Pockets, and his study of time values through walking, singing, and Clap-touch, are repeatedly combined with rhythmic bowing on the open string of a violin or cello. (This use of the open string in early studies is a sound introduction to fingerboard instruments because it avoids the use of the fingers that involves too many coordinations for the beginner. Leopold Auer believed that the whole first year of a child's string study should concentrate on these open-string exercises in rhythm to develop the bow-arm, which is to the string player what the breath is to the singer.)

Similarly, the interval studies, first on the Floor Staff and later in the Game of Leaps on an instrument, form a background for the study of the strings, which depend so rigorously on the ability to move from interval to interval with speed and accuracy.

One of the great shortcomings in class teaching of strings has been the inability to cope with the problem of playing in tune (intonation). Most string students are so involved in groping for notes that they do not hear the sounds they make, and once this habit of non-listening is acquired, years of remedial work can hardly repair the damage. Yet with the constant ear-training that is a part of almost every game in this book, young students are ready to undertake string studies with the solid foundation of Knowing How to Listen.

The finger games, which strengthen small muscles and prepare the child for holding the bow; the flash-card games and other activities which develop instantaneous responses; the staff games which gradually acquaint the eyes, the ears, and the body of the child with the treble and bass staves—and eventually with the tenor and alto as well—in fact, the total contents of this book form a logical and solid foundation for the study of strings (no less than of other instruments).

Even with this background, however, under the conditions of present-day education, there are defects in the available methods for teaching the strings. These would not have been defects in a society that believed in strict disciplines, forced practicing, and ambitious goals. The Heifetz and Elman who grew up in an earlier generation had parents with no more compunctions about making their children practice than about making them learn the multiplication tables. Children then were forced to practice until such a time as their own fluency at the instrument offered its own inducements.

With the permissive ways of modern child-rearing, however, there can be no forcing. Children of today are not fired with the ambition to be great soloists—somehow they know the score, the lifetime of practice slavery. Two conditions must take the place of compulsion. First, the subject must be made attractive enough to beckon the child along the path of study. Pretty pictures in the text are no answer, but rather a thorough understanding of fundamental principles from the beginning. Second, the children need to know the thrill of making music with others in a social experience, and they need to feel this exhilaration from the start. The public schools should provide opportunities for music-making for the greenest beginner. It should be possible for a seven- or eight-year-old to play along with the school orchestra or band in specially written open-string—or barely more difficult —parts to fit some of the orchestra's repertory. Without such early persuasions as these, modern children cannot be expected to work their way through to competence on the strings.

There have been many attempts to make string study more attractive, but in general they do not offer the child a firm enough grasp of the instrument. He wants security and clarity. Beginners on string instruments are apt to be in the dark for years. When they look at their fingerboard, what do they see? Only blackness. They do not see clearly what the piano beginner sees at the first lesson: a neat division of the keyboard into half steps. One almost shrinks from further comparisons. How different, for example, is the immediate response of a pressed piano key from the groping for a note on a fingerboard!

It is this total darkness that frustrates the string beginner and is the chief deterrent to continued study. The beginner grows weary and frightened at the prospect of remaining so long in a dark passageway. Yet there is a way out. It is possible to teach strings with stability and lucidity even in the early stages.

117

INTRODUCTION TO THE FINGERBOARD

In mathematics, we find the unknown by proceeding from the known. Let us now say,

Given: four open strings

This is a tangible reality. We can present all the notes of the instrument in their relation to these existing and easily recognized realities—the G, D, A, and E strings on the violin, the C, G, D, and A strings on the viola and cello. Considering the open string as the lowest note of an interval, each note playable on each string can be thought of as being a specific interval above the open string on which it lies. Even a class in general musicianship can absorb this concept.

The same class can learn still another concept which escapes many a string student in his first year. One shortens the vibrating length of a string by placing one's finger on that string. This is known as "stopping" the string. Set in motion, the string vibrates freely from the bridge to the firmly placed finger. The shorter the string, the higher the pitch. When we speak later of double stops, we mean that two strings are stopped simultaneously. Some beginners' squeaking comes from faulty bowing, but a good deal comes from faulty stopping of the string. Beginning students should at all times be led to experiment and find these things out for themselves. When they squeak, for example, they should turn detective and decide for themselves whether it was the fault of the fingers' not stopping the vibration firmly or of the bow's slipping too near the bridge.

The first term of string study, then, should be spent in becoming acquainted with the four open strings, and how they are "stopped" to produce higher pitches; in getting the bow-arm moving freely in varied rhythmic patterns; in learning a few simple pieces to be played in a group or separately with a minimum vocabulary of fingered notes; and in playing along with the school orchestra or band if possible. The pupils are now ready to begin to study the fingerboard in more detail.

The objective of this stage of study should be to develop a concept of notes through a unified association—as the child hears them, sings them, sees them on paper, and locates them on the fingerboard. The primary task is coordination of ear training, eye training, and muscle training, combined with a "fingerboard sense" into reflex-like responses.

Perhaps the greatest fault of present-day methods is Overlooking the Obvious. Consider the diagrams of the fingerboard in every beginning method: the numbers usually refer to the fingers; but as new fingers or new keys are used, the whole look of the diagram changes. If letter names are used instead, these too change when new notes, new strings, and new positions are introduced. Nor is a fret system or chart pasted on the fingerboard the answer, for these are but crutches.

What the child needs is a clear, unchanging map of the territory he is about to explore.

The Fingerboard Ear Training Charts reproduced in Figures 31--33 provide such a guide. For since these map the fingerboard in terms of interval steps rather than fingering, they never change. They are a basic tool for the study of stringed instruments.

These Fingerboard Charts should not merely be distributed to string students and occasionally consulted. They should be created slowly as the coordinations themselves are developed. They should evolve out of the children's own experience in hearing, seeing, and measuring intervals as these are absorbed into every learning fibre. First the exploration, the experience, the acute listening and singing for comparison; then the charting under the guidance of the teacher. It is the concept behind the chart that matters. The ingraining of the concept must proceed slowly, as the charting itself progresses slowly—over the first few years of study.

The following section shows how the chart is developed and how its use cultivates habits of second-nature muscular responses that leave the attention free to consider truly musical problems of phrasing, dynamics, tempo, form, tone production, and so forth.

119

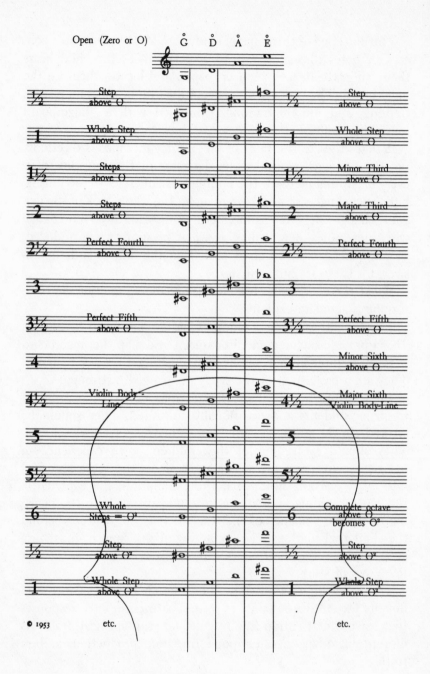

Fig. 31. Fingerboard Chart: Violin

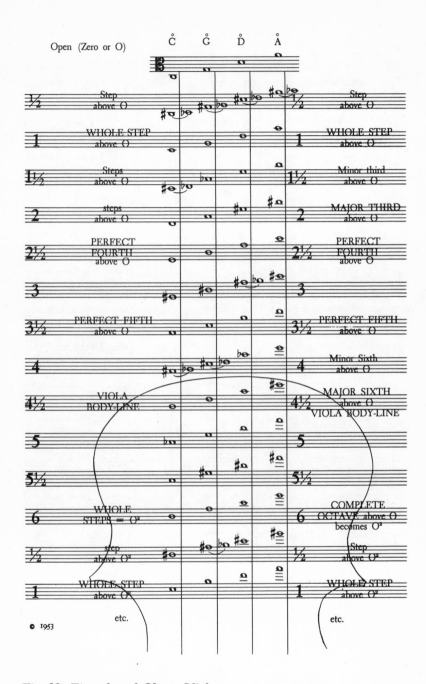

Fig. 32. Fingerboard Chart: Viola

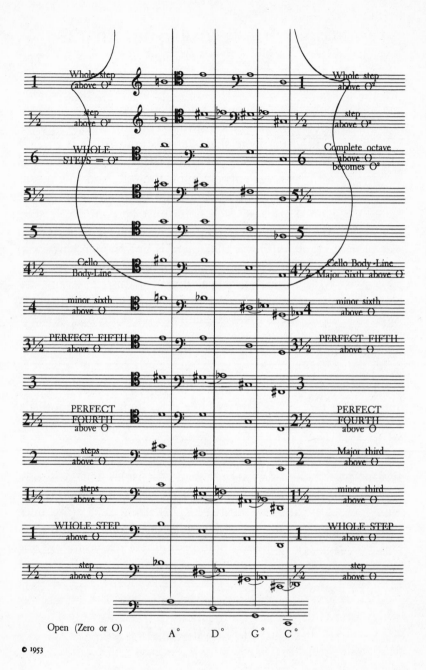

Fig. 33. Fingerboard Chart: Cello (read up from bottom)

BUILDING THE FINGERBOARD CHARTS

Since the half step is the unit of division of occidental music and the piano keyboard is a visual example of this division, it is logical to chart the violin, viola, and cello fingerboards in terms of half-step progressions up each string. This the teacher and pupils do together, using large sheets of posterboard. It is a year's project. For there are no frets or keys on these string instruments; the fine adjustments rely entirely upon the ear. And this means that the charted half steps up from the open string must not merely be learned visually; each note must be continually sung and constantly heard in its relation to the open string on which it is placed. Hindemith says that there is not enough singing in our harmony classes. The omission of constant singing for comparison and for intonation development is also a serious deficiency in our string classes. For the instrument can be thought of as merely the extension of the child's own voice box, the bow as an extension of his breath.

In the early stages of study the intervals are charted in half-step progression from the open string—which we call "open" or "zero" (0)—to the octave above. This, in turn, becomes a new home base or zero (0^2) for further measurements of intervals. These measurements in the second octave only duplicate those of the first, just as they do on the piano keyboard.

Charted in this way the upper reaches of the string instruments become familiar territory rather than No Man's Land. Surprisingly few students after even five or six years of training know the upper registers of any but the highest string. As a cellist once said, "I call the upper part of my cello the Bronx, because I always get lost there." There should be no more reason for a string player to feel lost in the upper registers than for a piano student to be dismayed by the last octave on the keyboard.

After dividing the fingerboard into half steps, the student becomes aware not only of the relationships between notes going up each string, but also of those *between notes lying horizontally across all four strings*. They must strive for a reflex-quick knowledge of both of these relationships.

123

The emphasis on fingerboard ear-training makes tangible, definite, and visible what has been elusive and hidden. It makes it possible for the child to grasp instead of to grope, for each note on the fingerboard now has a precise identification in relation to the open string. For example, since middle C on the G string is always 2½ steps above open G, it is referred to as "on the 2½-space." If a child is having difficulty playing middle C, the teacher can say, "That is on the 2½-space. Look at the note, find it on the chart, look at your fingerboard; now play and sing the open-string G; now sing A a whole step up, then B, another whole step up. You are now on the two space. (*The teacher points to the chart.*) Now a half step more—that's C. Now sing open G and then C, two and a half steps up. Play and sing: GABC. Sing G to C. Play G to C. Compare it with what you sang. What are the notes that lie in the same place across the strings? . . . etc . . . etc. . . ." (Compare to the study of intervals on the Floor Staff.)

All fingerings are referred to by ordinal numbers: first, second, third, and so forth, so that there is no confusion with the cardinal numbering of the interval spaces. The advantage lies in focussing the attention on the tone to be produced instead of on the fingering to be used—on results rather than means.

The charts also record one landmark which exists on every string instrument, though no text has ever brought it to the attention of the student. This is the Body Line (known to violin makers as the Purfling)—a thin ebony line, or inlaid border, that runs around the body of the instrument, close to the outer edge. It meets the neck of the instrument at approximately the 4½-space, or a major sixth up from the open string. This is made graphic by the rough sketch of the instrument on the Fingerboard Chart.

POSITIONS

Until recently, most violin students were taught to think in terms of "positions" (meaning positions of the left hand as it moves up and down the neck of the instrument). They were taught that they would feel most comfortable in the first, third,

124

and fifth positions, and that the second and fourth positions were to be avoided whenever possible. Students could be heard to ask one another, "What position are you studying now?" With the habits of thinking which this approach and these charts establish, these conventionally numbered positions need no longer be considered.

It is the contour of the musical phrase that is the ultimate factor deciding the fingering. The position is dictated by the fingering. The lowest note and the highest note of a phrase delineate the shape of the phrase, and that fingering is used which provides a smoothness and an economy of motion to encompass this contour. In other words, if there is no *special* effect to be made, there is no reason to jump from position to position if the notes can be reached comfortably from one position. The whole study of position for its own sake can be forgotten. This has several advantages: with the focus of attention on the shape of the phrase, there is greater flexibility and fluency in the playing; and the emphasis, once again, is not on the means but on the musical end. Furthermore, since in modern music we play more *in between* the old positions than in them, the concept of "positions" becomes increasingly meaningless.

PRACTICING

The beginner should have a clear idea of what to practice and how to practice it. For this purpose all basic string technique can be divided into four component parts, and with the exception of vibrato, all basic technical problems can be fitted into one of these four categories. They are:
1 Bowing
2 Trills
3 Shifts
4 Double Stops
With this approach, the student becomes aware from the outset that every piece can be broken down into all the necessary technical studies simply by analyzing the relationships between each two notes. Any problems concerning these relationships will fall into one of the above categories. The student should early

learn how to diagnose and how to remedy, thus achieving self-reliance by knowing how to work his way from difficulty to mastery.

Bowing

If there is a difficulty of bowing—an awkward string change, for example, or uneven tone production, or incorrect rhythmic division of the bow—the problem should be stripped of all fingering and isolated to the open strings where the attention can be concentrated on the bowing itself. Although a detailed exposition of method is beyond the scope of this section, the general principle is that the string changes and the rhythmic bow-divisions involved in most cases can be mastered by a practicing device that takes the problem from each string to every other string. On the violin, the progression would be as follows:

G to D, G to A, G to E (G is home base)
D to G, D to A, D to E (D is home base)
A to G, A to D, A to E (A is home base)
E to G, E to D, E to A (E is home base)

with corresponding strings for the viola or cello. This routine exploits all the possibilities, and develops control of the bow arm. (For other studies in the rhythmic control of the bow, see Measure Pockets, page 61.)

Trills, Shifts, Double Stops

These three categories comprise the left-hand technique. For practicing purposes, fingering problems can be analyzed by the student and placed in one of these three categories:

1. If two notes lie on the *same string within one hand position,* make a trill exercise of them, starting with half notes, repeating the two notes as quarters, then as eighths, triplets, sixteenths, etc. (Compare with the Dance of the Fingers, page 41.)

2. If the two notes lie on the same string but *not within reach of one position of the hand,* make a shifting exercise of them, using every possible fingering. (Compare with the Game of

126

Leaps, page 76.) The same permutation principle described in the bowing routines can be followed here, using every finger as home base for the shift to every other finger thus:

1st finger to 1st finger; 1st to 2nd; 1st to 3rd; 1st to 4th
2nd finger to 1st finger; 2nd to 2nd; 2nd to 3rd; 2nd to 4th
3rd finger to 1st finger; 3rd to 2nd; 3rd to 3rd; 3rd to 4th
4th finger to 1st finger; 4th to 2nd; 4th to 3rd; 4th to 4th

Allow no sloppy slides but aim for lightning movement and bull's-eye accuracy.

3. If the notes are on adjacent strings, make a double-stop study of them.

Most students have Double-stop Phobia. One violinist remembers that, as a child, if she was offered a choice of new pieces, she always looked them over hastily and chose the one with the fewest of these abominations. Yet there is no reason why the beginner should not become familiar with double stops as soon as he has acquired some control of open-string tone production and some facility in bowing. Single notes will be better understood because they will acquire a meaningful relation to all surrounding notes. The key to understanding comes in expanding the statement with which the study of the Fingerboard Charts began:

Given: four open strings—*tuned in perfect fifths.*

In other words, the interval of a perfect fifth or 3½ steps exists between any two adjacent strings at any point. Every double stop that is not a fifth itself will be either a specific number of half steps *more* than a perfect fifth or *less* than a perfect fifth. When the student assimilates this fact, most double-stop difficulties vanish.

Even a beginner can place one finger on two strings and thereby produce a perfect fifth. Using this interval as a basis, the teacher can help the child build other double stops. If he adds a half step to the higher string, for example, he has a minor sixth. If he adds a whole step, he has a major sixth. As he continues to build up the pitch of the upper string, he soon realizes that the octave is always the original perfect fifth (3½ steps) plus 2½ steps more (3½ and 2½ equal 6, and an octave's 12 half steps equal 6 whole steps). Even fingered octaves (the bugbears of many a string player) lose their forbidding character once this concept is absorbed.

Again, starting with the perfect fifth, the beginner builds up the pitch of the lower string. Now he is contracting the interval, making it smaller than its 3½ steps.

This practice on the instrument is accompanied by constant singing and a good deal of experimentation in different sections of the fingerboard. With the younger pupils, most attention is paid to the simplest intervals, the perfect fifths, the sixths, the perfect fourths, the thirds, but sooner or later all the intervals are brought into this building of double stops. The child is not learning one particular double stop in one particular piece or exercise, but is making the acquaintance of the whole tribe. (Compare with Interval Hopscotch and Interval Hopscotch with Partners, pages 91 and 92.)

From the study of trills, shifts, and double stops, it is a natural step to the advanced study of double-stop trills and double-stop shifts, since these are merely elaborations of the basic elements already mastered.

Vibrato

The introduction of vibrato is not usually made in the first two years, nor is its use imperative in a grade-school orchestra. Once the basic elements are integrated, however, the vibrato can be developed in a simple manner, through rhythmic control of the movements of the left arm and wrist in a routine similar to the trill exercise: first one tremor to a beat, then two, then three and finally four, in every instance followed by three counts of complete relaxation. It is important to master both wrist vibrato and arm vibrato, the former for singing tone (cantilena), the latter for double stops, chords, and a more intense tone. Since, in vibrato, the arm is completely relaxed, its use assures the avoidance of strain. (Compare with the sensation experienced in Hanging On to the Boat, page 39.)

SUMMARY

It should be apparent by now that this approach to string instrument study sets the pupil in a creative and exploratory role. He discovers the problems and learns how to work out their solutions himself. The teacher is but the guide to the child's exploration. As the study progresses, teacher and pupil together write a textbook based on all the primary elements discussed above, but specifically directed toward each pupil's individual needs. The teacher's aim should be no Procrustean bed that attempts to fit every pupil to the same methods, but rather an individual method for each child.

The teacher should encourage the child to create his own studies. Each cook appreciates his own cooking; and it is more agreeable to practice one's own *creations* than somebody else's *dry technical exercises*. Building exercises through chromatic progressions up the entire fingerboard not only develops fluency and efficiency but, since the exercises are the child's own inventions, and based on elements in the pieces he himself is studying, they are more meaningful to him. Naturally, the study is done in small doses; but with each day's practice involving some fresh exploration, the accumulation of technique at the end of a year is impressive.

With these simple rock-bottom essentials, string instrument study can still have a future, even in this day of limited practice time. Without intensive dedication, there can be no professional career; but with a modest efficiency on the instrument, the student can easily share the enriching experience of community music-making.

FINGERBOARD LOTTO

MATERIALS: One Fingerboard Chart for each player; transparent plastic or cellophane disks about ¾" in diameter; flash cards, each with one note from the chart; pencils.

This is a version of the familiar game of lotto (or bingo) for younger string students. A section of the Fingerboard Chart corresponds to the bingo card (for beginners, the section from zero up to the 3½-space should be sufficient). To make each card different, each child chooses one interval space across all four strings as out-of-bounds for him. This he covers with a pencil, and his play is confined to the rest of the "card." (This is a useful pedagogical device since it takes advantage of that human perversity that finds most interest in "forbidden" things. If the 2-space on a child's card is out-of-bounds, this is almost a guarantee that he will learn the 2-space notes first.)

The game progresses in the usual bingo style, the players covering, with their disks, the notes that are flashed on the cards. The first to have covered four notes across all four strings wins. For more experienced students the field of play can be extended to more and more intervals, and the number of notes to win can be increased to eight, twelve, or sixteen.

During the progress of the game, it is essential to produce the sound of each note, both vocally and instrumentally, with special reference to the open string on which it lies.

THE GAME OF FINGERBOARD

MATERIALS: The game board—a large Fingerboard Chart, pasted on cardboard; transparent disks or buttons, one of a different color for each player; a cardboard and metal spinner (these come with many children's games) with the following pasted in place of the original numbers: ½ (half step); 1 (whole step); 1½ (minor third); 2 (major third); 2½ (perfect fourth); 3 (augmented fourth or diminished fifth); 3½ (perfect fifth).

This is a game for students of ten years of age or more, to familiarize them with the entire fingerboard. It can be played with pleasure and profit during rest periods between stretches of practicing.

The Game of Fingerboard resembles parchesi, with home represented by the bottom note of the bottom string (that is, the G—or 0—of the open G string) and the goal an octave above the highest open string (that is, the E an octave above the open E string—or 0^2—of the E string).

The players sit in the same relation to the game board as they would to the actual instrument in performance. In other words, in the case of the violin or the viola, they sit so that the body of the instrument, as sketched on the chart, is close to the players, with the strings stretching away from them to the (unsketched) pegs; in the case of the cello, they sit so that the pegs are closest to them, with the body of the instrument farthest away. Only three or four can play at any one board.

Each player in turn takes a spin, and moves his disk the required number of steps. He has a choice, however: he may move down, up, or across. The object, like that in parchesi, is twofold: 1) to send the other players home (back to open G) by landing on the same space as their men; and 2) to reach the goal (E-0^2).

The player wins an extra spin if he lands either on the 4½-space (the Body Line of the instrument); on the 6-space (an octave above open, or 0^2); or on one whole step above 0^2.

The game should be played with an instrument at hand. Then each note can be checked for intonation by plucking an open

131

string on which the note can be played, and singing the indicated interval, before the finger is placed on the string. Through playing the Fingerboard Game in this way, the students absorb not only the notes in half-step progressions up each string but also, and what is more valuable, the notes in fifths across all four strings. Furthermore, the premium spins encourage them to explore the higher positions on each string, and to become familiar with the valuable landmark of the instrument's Body Line.

For older pupils, a more complete Fingerboard Chart can be used, which makes it possible to set the goal as the second octave above the highest open string (E-0^3).

INDEX

135

136

137

138

Set in Linotype Electra
Format by John Rynerson
Manufactured by The Haddon Craftsmen, Inc.
Published by HARPER & BROTHERS, *New York*

Date Due

11-13-56			
AUG 2 '57			
JAN 2 '58			
1-27-58			
OCT 2 9 '58			
JAN - 8 '59			
5/62			
JUL 3 '62			
FEB 24 '63			
MAR 9 '63			
APR 3 '63			
MAR 5 '64			
JAN 1 4 '65			
JAN 2 5 '65			
OCT 5 1968			
JAN 1 9 1971			
Ⓖ	PRINTED	IN U. S. A.